Grammar in the
Construction of Texts

Open Linguistics Series

The *Open Linguistics Series*, to which this book makes a welcome contribution, is 'open' in two senses. First, it provides an open forum for works associated with any school of linguistics or with none. Linguistics has now emerged from a period in which many (but never all) of the most lively minds in the subject seemed to assume that transformational-generative grammar—or at least something fairly closely derived from it—would provide the main theoretical framework for linguistics for the foreseeable future. In Kuhn's terms, linguistics had appeared to some to have reached the 'paradigm' stage. Reality today is very different. More and more scholars are working to improve and expand theories that were formerly scorned for not accepting as central the particular set of concerns highlighted in the Chomskyan approach—such as Halliday's systemic theory, Lamb's stratificational model and Pike's tagmemics—while others are developing new theories. The series is open to all approaches, then—including work in the generativist–formalist tradition.

The second sense in which the series is 'open' is that it encourages works that open out 'core' linguistics in various ways: to encompass discourse and the description of natural texts; to explore the relationships between linguistics and its neighbouring disciplines such as psychology, sociology, philosophy, artificial intelligence, and cultural and literary studies; and to apply it in fields such as education and language pathology.

The present volume makes a significant contribution to the series' interest in discourse and text. It illustrates the way in which language items that have till recently been thought of as part of 'sentence grammar' may be insightfully seen as specified by—or even as part of—an eventual holistic grammar of discourse.

Open Linguistics Series Editor
Robin P. Fawcett, The Polytechnic of Wales

Modal Expressions in English, Michael R. Perkins
Text and Tagmeme, Kenneth L. Pike and Evelyn G. Pike
The Semiotics of Culture and Language, eds: Robin P. Fawcett, M. A. K. Halliday, Sydney M. Lamb and Adam Makkai
Into the Mother Tongue: A Case Study in Early Language Development, Clare Painter
Language and the Nuclear Arms Debate: Nukespeak Today, ed: Paul Chilton
Functional Approaches to Writing: Research Perspectives, Barbara Couture
The Structure of Social Interaction: A Systemic Approach to the Semiotics of Service Encounters, Eija Ventola
New Developments in Systemic Linguistics, Vol. 1: Theory and Description, eds: M. A. K. Halliday and Robin R. Fawcett

Grammar in the Construction of Texts

Edited by
James Monaghan

 Frances Pinter (Publishers), London

First published in Great Britain in 1987 by
Frances Pinter (Publishers) Limited
25 Floral Street, London WC2E 9DS

British Library Cataloguing in Publication Data

Grammar in the construction of
texts.—(Open linguistics series)
1. Discourse analysis
I. Monaghan, James II. Series
410   P302
ISBN 0-86187-627-X

Typeset by Joshua Associates Limited, Oxford
Printed by SRP Ltd, Exeter

Contents

Foreword

This preface is an introduction to an introduction, in the sense that I can only overlay my own view of language research on top of such a wide diversity of papers. As an old hand in matters of struggling with sentences in texts, I look with approval on the various contributors here who tackle the nitty-gritty of sentences in written and spoken language without being too constrained by any of the well-known linguistic theories. Such an apparently short-sighted view may raise eyebrows—as if it were the blind telling the blind to grope along, with both hands feeling out the linguistic contours of texts and transcripts.

In my view the Information Technology revolution has brought very serious challenges to modern linguistics, one which is the recent advance in the technology for the storage of texts. Some of the chapters in this book point to interesting ways in which linguists may increasingly use such corpora. To the discourse analyst all words are important. But some are more important than others, and they are all those words which signal discourse structural meanings. My term for this is the *metalanguage* (of English here).

What is really needed is the established facts of communicative behaviour of *all words* of the English language, not just the obvious closed-system words. It is now the late twentieth century and we are very, very far away from such a desirable goal.

Here we all are, each one of us struggling to master our chosen part of real language. If we are to make a dent in the fast-growing information crises which are crowding in on us, then we need far more of what we see in this volume. We need careful studies of actual language use in all possible situations, with the view of establishing the linguistics of the communicative consensus, so that we can put some real language into artificial intelligence.

I am in fact understating the case. We in linguistics are faced with the challenge from all potential users of databases, not to mention the future computer which is supposed to be going to be able to communicate in natural language. In my view, the Alvey effort has proved inadequate in its handling of the research required for so-called natural language. What we need is something like the team effort that President Kennedy produced for the space race to the Moon. It would mean tackling the nitty-gritty of language as seen in this volume, but on a much vaster scale. If by 'linguistics' we mean a study of how language actually works, our future credibility depends on its success. Above all, we need the scope for new theories of language operation which such a vast enterprise should yield.

Eugene Winter, Hatfield Polytechnic

1 Introduction

James Monaghan,
The Hatfield Polytechnic

Unlike areas of research with a longer tradition within modern linguistics, textual studies is a child of the communications revolution that occurred in the middle of the twentieth century. This means that the workers in this field have almost always had good and quick access to results from their colleagues elsewhere. In consequence, there have not developed the hermetically sealed schools of thought that characterized, say, syntax or phonology in the 1940s and 1950s. So, while the authors of the chapters in this volume represent most of the European countries with a major tradition in this area, and while there are in one sense several main themes to this collection, we will repeatedly note the complementarity of interests, methods and conclusions throughout.

The developments in information technology in the 1970s and early 1980s, as well as stimulating intellectual contact, have also meant that linguistics has been enriched by new and more sophisticated technology for sound recording and computing, so that areas of study can be approached that were beyond the reach of unaided researchers. One only has to think of the labours needed to produce dictionaries, concordances and lists of collocations using only filing cards—not to mention the process of calculating linguistic statistics—to realize how far computer technology, with its power to handle large data bases of natural language texts, is revolutionizing the field. Similarly, the use of portable audio- and video-recording equipment and the development of technologies of sound analysis have opened up the study of naturally occurring speech in a way that was not possible in the days when transcriptions had to be depended on as prime records of the data. The fruits of these modern techniques are amply demonstrated in this collection.

All of the contributors to this volume have considerable experience in the study of natural language texts and the only condition laid on them was that their chapters should reflect such work, rather than more theoretical questions. Not that there is any implied criticism of pure theoretical research into problems such as the nature of text in general, but it was felt that a concentration of effort would benefit the book as a whole. Furthermore, as the reader will soon see, practical discussion of real data does not detract from the theoretical sophistication of the subsequent analysis and the wider-reaching insights it provides. The authors were not restricted as to method or theoretical approach, so long as their contribution was based on the study of naturally occurring texts. The result is a focussed set of papers with a stimulating diversity of approach.

The diversity comes from the theoretical traditions that the various authors represent and from the fact that, like most students of text linguistics today, they do not treat the area as something divorced from linguistics in general, but rather as a study naturally growing from attention to specific points in phonology, grammar or lexis and in turn feeding new insights into each of these. Furthermore, the work reported here reflects the influences on linguistics from psychology, sociology and education as well as drawing on a wide spectrum of recent developments from within linguistics as such. All the papers, therefore, reflect the consensus attitude which will surely characterize the linguistics of the latter part of this century.

Three of the most important aspects of the consensus reflected in the chapters in this collection are the attention to the functioning of language structures, the importance given to testing theory in renewal of connection in reality, and the openness to theoretical insights which have their origins outside the bounds of core linguistics. The stress on meaning as function in context and the emphasis on the analysis of real texts recur throughout this volume. Only two authors do not include a discussion of specific text examples and in both cases the theoretical insights counterpoint text-based discussion of a similar topic elsewhere.

The articles in this collection are all based on papers delivered to the Hatfield Conference on Discourse Structure, which was organized by the Hatfield Polytechnic Linguistics Group in 1983 in cooperation with the British Association for Applied Linguistics (BAAL). My editorial material is designed to draw attention to links between the various contributions, and everything in those sections is my responsibility, including the errors. The only excuse for my intruding at all is to provide a setting and a map of the connections between chapters. For those who know more about texts than I do, the chapters will have lost no value from being taken on their own.

I have divided the collection into three main blocks, although the complementarity of the chapters is such that points of comparison override these boundaries. The first section, which I have called **Discourse structures**, contains five chapters looking at points of wide theoretical interest; the second section, **Conversational strategies**, consists of chapters on aspects of informal speech in one form or another; and the final section, **Comparative studies**, draws on insights from the study of texts in more than one language.

Finally, a word of thanks to all who made this book possible. As well as all the authors, I owe a great debt of gratitude to Robin Fawcett, general editor of this series, without whose good offices from start to finish of this project I would never have made it. I must also thank Winnie Crombie, Christine Cheepen and Colette Monaghan for reading various parts and improving my version of them, and Margaret Back and Christine Cheepen for retyping the manuscript.

Part I
Discourse structures

The four chapters in this section—Meyer on structural signals, Arndt on functional indicators, Hüllen on tense and time, and Lowe on causes and reasons—address questions concerning how the reader or hearer decodes the meaning of texts from linguistic signals within the textual and extra-textual context. All four focus attention on the characteristics of descriptive language, as distinct from, say, narrative or interactive speech, although their ideas have a wider application.

Meyer takes as his topic the way structure is signalled in technical discourse. He sees technical discourse as the prototype of all coherent discourse since the purpose of this text type can only be achieved by the decoder successfully comprehending the connections between the text elements, and between their real-world referents. This is surely correct within the confines of transactional language use, where some quantifiable goal beyond social interaction is being pursued. Arndt's classification of reportives as the naturally unmarked terms in his system of referential functions adds support to this position, as does Hüllen's discovery that what he calls PRESENT-texts, i.e. factual, expository texts, have much less adverbial specification than the PAST type. Because Hüllen does not confine his attention to one type of discourse, his paper nicely contextualizes the others. And, finally, Lowe's detailed discussion, from within as it were, of some of the ways similar clause relations are indicated by the lexico-grammar rounds off the group and serves as a bridge to the next section.

Like Lowe, Meyer also draws attention to something very similar to what Arndt calls functional indicators, linguistic configurations aiding the interpretation of utterances in social interaction. We will return to Arndt and Lowe, but it is interesting to note here Meyer's very functionalist definition of structure. Whereas it has been fashionable in some quarters to contrast form and meaning, Meyer sees meaning as inherent in the structure. Before an apparent regularity can be counted as structural, it must have a function in the text. Structural meaning is part of text meaning and it can be signalled by formal regularities. Some apparent regularities, however, have no function and some functional connections have no signals other than co-occurrence. Meyer, then, sees discourse semiotics as the relationship between the structural signal and its functional interpretation.

The transactional nature of technical writing requires high functional density and little redundancy, with a priority on signalling coherence. One reason why this is regarded as one of the most typical written forms of discourse is that, in literate societies, the most common reaction to a complex set of facts is to write them down. This applies both to the encoder and the decoder in situations such as the classroom. The teacher will at least jot down headings so as to 'order his thoughts' with a view to expressing his ideas in the most efficient way, and the student will be likely to take notes. In fact, it is a difficult task to restrain literate students from withdrawing from discussion to write things down. This behaviour goes a long way to explaining why non-literate cultures often resist literacy. The spectacle of literates trying to relate efficiently in speech alone, as when they have to give and remember coherent directions in the street, lends credence to the criticism that literacy leads to the memory atrophying. At the very least, it deprives speakers of oral strategies for storing large amounts of speech data efficiently.

The second part of Meyer's paper makes use of the classification of signs into icons, indexes and symbols to discuss specific types of structural signal. He sees lexical cohesion as indexical because it is a by-product of topic oriented text production. In other words, lexical cohesion in this type of text is seen as primarily exophoric. There is obviously a lot in this. Nevertheless, the role of endophora should not be underestimated, even in technical discourse. Many items in the text are only interpretable with the initial help of other textual items. Most well documented is the role of endophoric lexical items such as *problem*, *solution*, *contrast*, etc., which I have called 'referentially unfulfilled lexical items' (Monaghan 1985: 378–9).

As Meyer himself would put it, a structural signal derives in the case of these words from a syntagmatic relation between a lexical meaning and a sentence meaning. These words, and also, at a more abstract level, words like *experiment*, *proof*, *theory*, are important ways in which the author of a text imposes regularity on the description of what has taken place, what Firth calls 'the general mush of goings-on'. Such words also help the decoder make connections between events and objects (or more immediately between linguistic tokens representing them) whose relatedness is not culturally self-evident, that is, presupposed by the collocational range of the linguistic tokens themselves. In other words, expository texts can be said to expand our experience of the world by altering our perceptions of the relationship between linguistic signs at various levels.

Referentially unfulfilled lexical items, which do not refer to inherent classes of item existent apart from the text, are crucial in this process, and Meyer makes a similar point with regard to conjunction which he points out is conventional, not indexical, in the sense that it is not given by the nature of reality but is part of the text-producer's encoding decisions. Although speakers often have ready-made conjoined phrases which are difficult to resist even where we would be hard pressed to justify them—such as *poor but honest* or *blonde and beautiful*—more often the choice between conjoining and disjoining is encoded in terms of the expectations of the interlocutors or even of the speaker alone. This latter case often obtains in texts intended to persuade.

The importance of the encoder's image of reality in the production of texts is to be seen in several ways. One is non-ideational coherence, and another is non-fulfilment above the lexical level. Meyer rightly draws attention to the way a coherent field of discourse is reflected by collocation in the lexical items used. As I have said, this cohesion is enhanced by the use of referentially unfulfilled lexical items which indicate the logical structure of the build-up of the argument. Parallel to this, however, is the interactional signalling of evaluation and formality which, even in expository texts of the kind under discussion, is important in maintaining the unity of the text. In face-to-face interaction, especially that involving more than one speaker, this can be much more complex, but also much more significant. Not only do items like *problem* and *solution* already contain their own element of evaluation, because nothing is a problem in itself—although only those things which have potential solutions can be so classified—but evaluative expressions like *better* and *logical* also supply lines of cohesion as well as defining situational–textual atmosphere.

Four paragraphs ago, I used the sentence *There is obviously a lot in this.* This is a perfect example of a sentence without referential exponents which can be identified in the real world. It is positively evaluative of the previous sentence and as such fits well with my positive evaluation of Meyer's paper as a whole, which in turn fits well with the expected attitude of an editor to a hand-picked selection from a group of submitted articles. The sentence can only be fully understood by being taken in all the sorts of contexts containing it and this not only establishes text to fulfil the pronouns, but also requires contextualization of the quantifier *a lot*.

Hüllen's paper on the English tense system also takes a firmly contextualist line. Tenses are to be interpreted in their environment of cotextual time denotation (especially adverbial specification) and situational factors (what Hüllen calls 'exophoric reference'). Both these points are worth repeating because until recently they had been consistently ignored in sentence-based grammars, especially those in the US (neo-) structuralist tradition. Hüllen's main interest is in everyday spoken discourse, but his approach is able to handle much more complex nested systems of embedded temporal contexts, like the kinds found in reported speech in historical narrative. Hüllen's main concern in this paper is to review the only two analytic tense forms in English, the 'present' and the 'past'. He sees them both as 'zero-tenses' in terms of temporal deixis and proposes that their primary function is to indicate the illocutionary quality dominating the text of which they are a part. Dependent on whether past or present tenses predominate, the text fulfils different functions as an extended speech act. Present tense highlights psychological immediacy and relevance to reality. Past tense distances the text from reality and is much more likely to have its concrete time reference expressed through adverbials or exophora than the present tense. Only one in ten of the present-group of predicates show temporal specification, while one in four of the past-group do.

Now, Barbara Strang 1962 and David Crystal 1966 both speak of the non-temporal nature of the English present and the importance of time specification. What is particularly interesting here is the extension of the claim about non-temporality to the past tense and the closer examination of the relationship of specification to the particular tense form. If time deixis is primarily a function of the whole text, as Hüllen argues, then this releases the two syntactically simple tenses to express text-long interactional meaning. There is an interesting parallel here to the difference between phonemic analysis of sound structure and prosodic analysis. Instead of working with the smallest segment all the time and discussing variation in terms of these individual segments, a contextual approach to grammar allows the individual tense form to be placed in its general context of both immediacy and temporal deixis.

Arndt is interested in the functional roles of cognitive verbs in texts. Like Hüllen in his discussion of time deixis, Arndt sees the main clue to the interpretation of utterance function as lying in the context. Although he acknowledges his intellectual debt to Conversational Analysis and Austin, he has himself also developed some extremely interesting parallels to Systemic Linguistics. Like the other authors in this section, he sees the production of text as producing a complex of interlocking meanings. He applies the notion of Functional Indicators, lexical, structural or intonational configurations which help to signal the function, or intended function, of an utterance in social interaction. Cognitive verbs are described in their role as Functional Indicators, i.e. in terms of their secondary meanings which refer to the truth and certainty of certain stretches of text, or to the way the encoder wants these text stretches decoded and acted upon. Arndt offers a classification of language in terms of a system of referential functions into representative, expressive and regulative functions. Parallel to these are the interactional functions where the place in the textual sequence overrides the normal category. A whole text may be a directive or a report but not a reaffirmation. This global view, which sees the whole text as an extended speech act made up symphonically of smaller movements momentarily supporting or restraining the main flow of the message, is most enlightening. Arndt's discussion of the different meanings of the English word *know*, both in terms of English syntax and of translation equivalents in related languages, illustrates well the point that even in expository texts the encoder continually signals his level of personal commitment to the match between his words and reality.

In a similar way, Lowe, looking in detail at the two related logical sequence clause relations CAUSE and REASON, makes important distinctions between the two notions in spite of their similarity in signalling. REASON is much more a text-internal construct than CAUSE, because it presupposes reasoning. As a consequence of this, it is necessary to distinguish between reasons for actions and reasons for speech acts. In other words, REASON can be applied both exophorically and endophorically. The fact that the English language uses the same small set of functional indicators such as *because*, *so* and *if* allows very fine modulations of the perceived relationships, as with law-like and quasi-law-like causality as distinct from enabling or facilitating causality.

Overall, the discussion opens a wider perspective on the lay view that language is about the communication of ideas. If the notion of ideas is further differentiated, it is possible to derive insight from this. Starting from the language evidence for the existence of ideas—it is possible to distinguish between, firstly, what might be called referentially concrete ideas, where some object or happening or circumstance is encoded by the speaker, and, secondly, the idea of the relationship between each such encoded chunk— Lowe illustrates well the kinds of subtleties that can be encoded in the lexico-grammar here.

It is of interest to note, however, that not only referentially concrete ideas like *cow* or *run* or even *beauty* but also the relations between them can be lexicalized in the form of nouns, verbs and adverbs, so that they too are treated as existent, or reified. Many theories of lexical look-up underestimate the potential creativity of the speaker in this regard. The encoder's decision to present some aspect of experience as a cause produces from the linguistic point of view the expectation that at some point an effect will become apparent. The encoding of a reason, on the other hand, means that some happening, verbal or non-verbal, will be justified in terms of it; in other words, we are shown what mental processes the encoder has gone through in conceptually relating the happening and its relation. Thus, central meta-linguistic concepts like CAUSE and REASON have to be encoded in grammar or lexis while being essentially exophoric. Arndt's text example of the effect of free-fall on radio equipment nicely supports Lowe's contention that reasons for action can all be derived from reasons for speech acts, because reasons presuppose reasoning. The happening has to have been mentally processed to have or be a reason and if the concept is also verbalized this overlays the external necessities. Cause, on the other hand, is not so dependent on verbalization to be appreciated. Animals clearly appreciate cause but this does not demonstrate that they can reason.

2 Some observations on the signalling of structure in technical discourse

Paul Georg Meyer

Bibliography of Linguistic Literature, Frankfurt am Main, West Germany

The problem of structure signals in technical discourse has attracted wide attention in diverse fields of linguistic research, such as stylistics, composition theory, reading research, language teaching for SP, automatic text processing, and documentation. Common to all such approaches is an interest in practical problems of the processing of technical information, either intellectual or machine-aided. English being the most widespread lingua franca of international scientific communication, it is on English technical discourse that the bulk of research has been conducted. This is in most cases done with an express hope thereby to facilitate the process of communication via English technical discourse, either by teaching students of science or humanities to read and write English more effectively, or by improving or economizing the process of documentation for technical literature.

My interest in this chapter is, *caveat lector*, not immediately practical. A more theoretically minded look at the problems of structure signals in general and at those in technical discourse in particular seems to me justified for two reasons: one is that practical applications of text-linguistic approaches in the fields of, for example, languages for specific purposes or machine-aided document description, can still profit from a deeper theoretical insight into the problems of technical discourse or discourse in general, since the models applied so far have been rather crude and unsophisticated, given the vast complexity of the structure of any discourse, even the most simple or stereotyped one. On the other hand, I believe that theoretical research in text linguistics can also profit considerably from an applicational perspective, particularly on technical discourse.

Technical discourse is not just one type of discourse among many others. It is the prototype of coherent discourse; that is our notions of coherence have been shaped on the model of technical, namely expository discourse. Narratives can be incoherent and still be good narratives because events or people's actions may be incoherent or difficult to see through. Incoherent expository discourse is just bad discourse; it simply does not fulfil its purpose. Expository discourse displays common-sense coherence in a pure, undiluted state, because it appeals to our common sense to get its message through. That is why to my mind the exploration of the regularities of technical discourse plays an essential part in the development of a theory of coherence.

This last point will not be elaborated further in this chapter; I hope to come back to it in the future. I will concentrate on confirming my first justification for a theoretical view on discourse structure, confident that 'nothing is more practical than a good theory'.

Let me begin by explaining the terms used in the title of this chapter. 'Technical discourse' is to be understood in a very broad sense here, comprising all sorts of (mostly written) discourse claiming some sort of common-sense coherence, and addressed to an anonymous, though more or less expert and specialized public. Apart from that, I will take the meaning of 'technical discourse' for granted.

A structure is any set of items with a set of relations between those items. Talking about discourse structure thus poses the problem of identifying the items and relations one is talking about. This is often not done with sufficient clarity in text linguistics. Often enough, some hazy notion of 'discourse structure' has been invoked, according to the well-known satirical motto, 'If you don't know what it is, call it a structure'. The items we shall be talking about in this chapter will be called text elements.

Syntagmatic relations between text elements are all relations of co-occurrence within a text, either in a predefined syntactic frame or without such constraints. A paradigmatic–syntagmatic relation within a text is a syntagmatic relation where the text elements involved can be viewed as having some kind of paradigmatic relationship in the linguistic system. A text ELEMENT may belong to the content plane or the expression plane of the text. Text elements of the content plane are, for example, lexical meanings, propositional meanings, illocutionary forces, etc. Text elements of the expression plane range from individual phonemes to macrosyntactic constructions. A text SEGMENT is always a bundle of text elements from both planes. In the case of individual phonemes or phoneme combinations, where the segmentation goes below morpheme level, elements from the content plane are usually missing in technical discourse. This is why the phonemic structure of technical discourse is next to irrelevant.

Text segments typically form hierarchies of smaller and larger segments, such as phoneme, lexeme, phrase, sentence, paragraph, chapter, text. But text elements can also be organized in a structure other than hierarchical. Certain text elements may recur at different places in a text and form a diffuse structure of text components. A good example of a diffuse structure is the meta-textual component of a text, which is as a rule not delimitable as a segment, but consists of a lot of recurring elements scattered over the whole text.

We have thus described roughly what sort of items and relations enter in discourse structure. The next question we must turn to now is: how can discourse structure be signalled?

This last question immediately poses the problem of MEANING. Signalling is necessarily a semiotic relationship, and this implies meaning. Any structure which does not have meaning is trivial enough, meaningless. It is not the structure as a formal mechanism that is interesting, it is the meaning of the structure. Note that this structural meaning is different from and should not be conflated with text meaning. It is part of the total meaning of the text, in much the same way as case roles are part of the total meaning of a sentence. And just as case roles can be signalled by syntactic relations, the meaning of discourse structure is signalled by syntagmatic and paradigmatic relations between text elements. We can thus see that our question was badly put: the semiotic relationship of signalling is not between the structure and something else; it is inherent in the structure. It is therefore not sufficient for a description of discourse structure to state the relevant items and their relationships. What is indispensable is a functional interpretation of the formal side of discourse structure. To give an example: simply stating that a certain lexical element recurs several times in a text is no serious contribution to a description of this text unless this recurrence is also given a functional interpretation, for example, that it signals a certain topical predominance of the objects referred to by the lexical item in question.

We can now define discourse structure as a set of relations (paradigmatic and/or syntagmatic) between text elements that are given a functional interpretation in the discourse.

Let us now investigate the semiotic relationship within discourse structure. It is, *nota bene*, not the relationship between discourse structure and something else, nor is it in particular the relationship between discourse and discourse meaning. It is the relationship between the formal side of a structure signal and its functional interpretation. Let me begin with a few characteristic examples. These will be the phenomena of rhyme, lexical cohesion, and conjunction.

How can RHYME be characterized in the framework sketched above? It is a recurrence of phonological elements, patterned according to certain rules which need not concern us here. It is a constrained syntagmatic–paradigmatic relationship between text elements on the expression plane, namely phonological elements. The relationship of recurrence is always syntagmatic–paradigmatic since it implies co-occurrence (= syntagmatic relation) AND identity of elements (= paradigmatic relation). But what is the meaning of rhyme? In a vague sense we may say that rhyme signals poeticity. But calling a text poetic is just another way of saying that it has certain formal characteristics, one of which may be rhyme. And it is nothing that could characterize texts uniquely. I am therefore tempted to say that rhyme signals nothing but itself. And this is, to my mind, the main reason why it is not used in technical discourse, as a rule. Rhyme may be used as a mnemonic device in pedagogic discourse, but this is a non-semiotic relationship: in this case rhyme does not signal the pedagogic intention, it only aids it. But in most cases rhyme is an end in itself and is therefore unsuitable for technical discourse. Technical discourse cannot afford redundancy. It has a high functional density: each text element has one or more functions-in-text. And since the overall function of technical discourse is not poetic, elements with a purely poetic function will not occur very frequently. The semiotic relationship inherent in rhyme being one of identity is thus an extreme form of ICONICITY: iconic signs resemble their referents, and what could resemble more than the referent itself?

Let us now take a look at LEXICAL COHESION.

Lexical cohesion is the patterned recurrence of lexical elements or semantic features in discourse. It is, therefore, again a paradigmatic–syntagmatic relationship, this time concerning elements of the content plane in discourse, that is lexical, meanings or their components. But what is signalled by lexical cohesion?

One could say that in poetic texts lexical cohesion again signals nothing but itself. But this is not true for technical discourse. In technical discourse, lexical cohesion signals thematic structure. The recurrence of certain lexical elements, or clusters of elements from narrow lexical fields in technical discourse, signals the field that the discourse is to be assigned to, gives hints at the predominant topics in it, and can also indicate a change of topic as the recurrence pattern changes from paragraph to paragraph. Since technical discourse is built on and around topics, lexical cohesion is a very important and characteristic element of structure in technical discourse. The semiotic relationship inherent in lexical cohesion, in so far as it indicates topical structure, is INDEXICAL in nature. This means that technical lexical cohesion is not constructed as such; it is a natural by-product of the process of topic-oriented text production.

To illustrate this, let me quote one of Halliday and Hasan's well-known examples: 'Wash and core six cooking-apples. Put them in a fire-proof dish.' The cohesive tie between 'cooking apple' and 'them' does not come about as a result of the author's intention to form a cohesive sequence of sentences by using the device of anaphoric reference. It is a by-product of the trivial fact that things mentioned in a recipe must be disposed of in some way or other, i.e. they must often be mentioned again. The rementioning of the apples is primarily a practical necessity; its linguistic 'regularity' derives from this. If this is true of anaphoric reference, it applies to lexical cohesion too. In other words, lexical cohesion, being indexical in nature, comes about not by virtue of linguistic rules, but by the necessities of the description of an object, of thematic progression. Technical discourse is always concerned with connections between objects. These connections are usually so complex that they cannot be explicated by simple proposition. Complex sentences and sentence sequences have to be formed. This necessarily leads to the repetition of acts of reference: the same object is referred to again and again. What is more, the connections being described are usually not completely beyond imagination. At least some of the objects involved must have some connection to each other in the reader's prior knowledge—and, thereby, in the lexical system of his language. Otherwise, the text would be incomprehensible to him. If the connection is less obvious, intermediate steps must be inserted which create a 'smooth' thematic progression. This is the whole secret of lexical cohesion, and of anaphora and substitution too.

Our last example of a structural device in discourse is CONJUNCTION. Conjunction is a purely syntagmatic relationship between two sentences or clauses and the conjunctive element. There is no necessary paradigmatic relationship, neither between the sentences nor with the conjunction itself.

The meaning of conjunction is linguistic meaning: it derives from the meanings of the elements involved. The relationship between conjunction and its meaning is, therefore, purely SYMBOLIC, i.e. conventional. The meaning of a conjunction comes about by virtue of conventional linguistic rules; knowing how to conjoin sentences is linguistic knowledge. Conjunction is to be regarded as an intentional act of the author. The formal device of conjunction is not a mere INDEX of the act of conjunction; it is the conventional MEANS of performing this act. On the other hand, lexical cohesion as such is not the MEANS of developing a theme; it is an INDEX of theme development.

We have thus ascertained the three classical types of signifying within discourse structure: iconic, indexical and symbolic (or conventional, as I would prefer). But there are two other possibilities of discourse structure: there may be structure signals that have no meaning (pseudo-structure or 'red herrings') and there may be structural meaning without overt expression. 'Red herrings' come into technical discourse by accident, author's incompetence or simply deception. Not every lexical repetition within discourse, for example, is significant; it may be mere coincidence. Not every 'cause', 'contrast', 'summary', 'argument' etc. labelled as such in technical discourse is really appropriate: such labels may even be deliberately misleading. But here we are leaving the domain of text linguistics proper and entering into stylistics or even literary criticism or composition marking (which is being done all the time anyway, often lacking methodological justification and reliability).

Structural meaning 'without' overt expression is a matter of degree. If we define our criteria for a structure signal rather loosely (as I would be inclined to do) we might enclose the syntagmatic relationship of mere juxtaposition among them.

In this case few, if any, cases of covert discourse structure would be left. 'Being in the same discourse' is certainly some kind of syntagmatic relationship; the problem is how to ascertain the exact functional meaning of this relation, if there is any. Consider the following example:

The lights have gone out. There must be a short circuit somewhere.

In this case there certainly is a relationship between the two sentences which has an important function in discourse. Inference from some effect on some obvious cause is a very common discourse mechanism which alone suffices to make a sequence of sentences coherent. There is no overt sign of this relationship in our example. Yet everybody acquainted with everyday phenomena of modern life such as electricity is able to supply the relationship from their knowledge. There is rather a 'thin' lexical cohesion (between 'light' and 'short circuit'). Its being there is no coincidence, given the familiarity of the causal relation involved: items causally connected in some way or other will always be in some kind of lexical affinity. But the causal (or any other) relationship will not always be so obvious. Consider:

(a) The accusatorial system is more adaptable than the inquisitorial one.
(b) It allows for practical changes in treatment methods to be introduced easily during the sentence.

Here we have some difficulty in defining the exact nature of the relationship between the sentences. Without entering into the causes–reasons debate, there are three different interpretations of sentence (b). It is (1) stating the cause for the truth of sentence (a); or (2) giving the reason for the author's choice of the adjective 'adaptable'; or (3) explicating the meaning of this same adjective. The reader's choice of interpretation depends on his prior knowledge and opinion. A reader may be (1) convinced that sentence (a) is true, but lack sufficient explanation for this fact; or (2) he may doubt whether sentence (a) is true, especially whether the adjective 'adaptable' is appropriate, and want something in the line of reasons for the author's claim; or (3) he may fail to appreciate fully the meaning of 'adaptable' in which case he may want further explication of this notion.

Lacking any overt sign of the exact relationship between the sentences, we are left with an unresolvable vagueness. The items of lexical cohesion merely indicate the broader field of discourse (legal matter), with no direct pertinence to the exact relationship between the sentences (not that this was the case with 'lights'–'short circuit' in our other example). We have gathered from our examples that there may be covert structure in technical discourse in the sense that sometimes overt signals do not allow any conclusions on the exact nature of a structural relationship. In this case the relationship must be supplied from the reader's knowledge or remain vague and open to interpretation.

Lexical cohesion and conjunction have been our main examples to illustrate some important differences between types of structural elements in discourses. Conjunction is a purely syntagmatic relationship which organizes sentences hierarchically into larger units. Lexical cohesion is a paradigmatic–syntagmatic relationship between word meanings which tends to form components rather than segments, though often changes in lexical cohesion may set off text segments from each other. Common to both phenomena is that they concern elements from the content plane of the text. To these must be added paradigmatic–syntagmatic relations between sentence meanings such as paraphrase and inclusions which have an important function in the organization of discourse. There are also lexical elements which by their very presence give a distinct functional meaning to sentences in discourse, such as *cause*, *contrast*, etc.; that is, a syntagmatic relation between a lexical meaning and a sentence meaning acquires the status of a structure signal.

Anaphoric reference is another example of conventional signalling of discourse structure. It is a linguistic means of taking up a topic again, and certain types of anaphora (including anaphora by lexical cohesion) correlate with certain types of thematic development.

There are other phenomena that concern elements from the expression plane. It has repeatedly been observed, for example, that certain syntactic configurations indicate structural features in technical discourse. Marked sentence patterns such as clefts, pseudo-clefts, or rhetorical questions may indicate a change of topic. Changes in morphosyntactic continuity such as change of tense, voice, aspect, mood, modality or number may indicate segment boundaries in discourse. Often a collocation of a syntactic and a lexical element is needed to make a structure signal. That-sentences, for example, in connection with certain delocutives or performatives are among the most prominent expressions of the meta-textual (and inter-textual) component.

To sum up, we have shown that discourse signals can come from all linguistic levels on both the content and the expression plane. They all interact to form the pattern of discourse which is a prerequisite to its comprehension. If discourse was an unstructured clew of expressions and meanings, nobody could extract any information from it. The more explicit the structure of a text is made, the easier is the reader's access to its meaning. The task of text linguistics in this context is to unravel the texture to find out how it works, and to provide a meta-language which helps to make our implicit comprehension of discourse explicit.

3 On denoting time in discourse

Werner Hüllen

Universität Gesamthochschule Essen, West Germany

3.0 There are at least two reasons for analysing how time is denoted in discourse. One is that the tense system, which is always involved in the denotation of time, belongs to the most important subsystems of language. There is hardly any utterance that does not employ it. So it must be looked upon as central to what happens when language is used, and is a linguistic problem in its own right. The other is that the way in which the tense system is described in grammars and taught in textbooks (and presumably in schools) is notoriously unsatisfactory. One supposed reason for this is that tense is never explained in texts and in discourse, but always in isolated and decontextualized sentences. This means that it is not explained in the context of communication but in the context of philosophical categories. If there is a need at all for a transphrastic description and analysis of language, it is here.

There is one attempt at explaining the tense system as a text organizing device which has become most influential in the linguistics of the Romance languages, though not, however, in linguistics devoted to the description of English. It is Harald Weinrich's book *Tempus. Besprochene und erzählte Welt* (1964).[1] My own analysis draws heavily on Weinrich's ideas, though I do not subscribe to all of them. One reason for this is that Weinrich in his book is really interested in the language of literature, whereas I am really interested in everyday discourse. This is why the following chain of thought will be illustrated with examples and an analysis of a section (1.6) from the *London–Lund Corpus of Spoken English* (Svartvik and Quirk 1980).

3.1 The denotation of time in a discourse is not brought about by the tense system alone but by exophoric reference, by adverbials AND by the tense system. I call 'exophoric reference' all semantic information and clues which a text provides in its message and which allows the receiver to apply or to add his own knowledge to them (Halliday and Hasan 1976: 31–7). Denotation of time is thus brought about by going back to the encyclopaedic information of language users. This can be dependent on or independent of the immediate situation in which partners in discourse confront each other. Examples from the *Corpus*:[2]

35 when he was in knickerbockers [unambiguous within the situation]
954 but he had been . . . educated in Russia before the Revolution [unambiguous within and outside the situation]

I call 'adverbials' all adverbs, prepositional phrases and temporal clauses which denote time in a text. It is their cooperation with the tense system which should arouse our special interest (Crystal 1966). As a rule, the tense system is described with the help of sentences in which adverbials occur just as tense forms do; but WHERE the denotation of time actually lies remains unanalysed. In such cases, the adverbials are used in order to disambiguate and identify the temporal meaning of the tenses. But grammarians hardly ask what 'share' tenses and adverbials (and exophoric reference) respectively have in denoting time. It is, however, important to raise this question, because everybody knows that there is no clear relationship between the tenses and time as we experience it as human beings. We all know that, for example, the present tense does not necessarily denote present time. So tense alone does not suffice to explain the denotation of predicates in this respect. Examples from the *Corpus*:

398 till he changes next year

In this case, the adverbial clearly marks the present as having future meaning.

742 he probably uses them other places

Here, the adverbial does the same though less clearly. These, of course, are well enough known facts. It remains to draw conclusions from them.[3]

3.2 There is unanimity that the most important tenses are PRESENT and PAST. From the point of view of discourse analysis this is so because these two tenses differentiate two basic types of texts (Weinrich 1964: *passim*). There are texts (of any length worth considering) which have predicates almost exclusively in the present and texts which have predicates almost exclusively in the past. The occurrence of, for example, present perfect or past perfect depends on the occurrence of present or past, but not the other way round. Thus we can speak of present-texts and past-texts, meaning that present and past have an essential function in organizing their coherence.

As a general characterization, we can call present-texts EXPOSITORY (discursive). The illocutionary force of their utterance is describing, stating, explaining, evaluating, arguing. These are not very clear labels; taken together, however, they do differentiate expository texts clearly from past-texts which we can call TELLING. The illocutionary force of their utterances is narrating or reporting. Expository texts are to be found in newspapers, in political speeches, in scholarly books, in business letters and private letters, in everyday conversations. Telling texts are to be found in narratives, in biographical or other reports which, of course, can again be found in conversations or letters. Often the two types are mixed. A historical report can, for example, be interspersed with arguing, explaining or evaluating passages, and a linguistic analysis can be interspersed with passages of historical reporting. In a normal case, it still remains clear what type of a text we basically have.

The difference between a present-text and a past-text, it follows from this, lies in what people do with them. The expository text in the present deals with facts; it is distinguished by psychological nearness. The speaker makes statements or disputes them; he speaks about the world. The listener gains new knowledge about reality. The telling text in the past deals with recollections or imaginings; it is distinguished by psychological distance. The speaker verbalizes what he has in mind; he speaks about a world in his head which may or may not have affinities with the real world. The listener takes the word of the speaker as the medium of experience.

The relations between the human subject and reality which are implied in these descriptions are, of course, to be understood from the point of view of naïve world knowledge, not of philosophical reflection.

It is my hypothesis that present and past do not denote any time at all *per se*, but that they serve as an indicator of the illocutionary quality that dominates the text. Though there are others, present and past are the strongest indicators of this kind, because they are obstinately repeated in every full sentence. Because of their neutrality to time, Weinrich proposed calling present and past 'zero-tenses'.

Examples from the *Corpus*:

1 Where do you come from
80 I don't know how much time Malcolm gets

Long stretches of discourse in the present may not denote any time at all, just as is the case for long stretches of discourse in the past. Temporal references, if needed, are supplied by the additional means mentioned, that is, by exophoric reference and by adverbials.

As hardly any texts exist which have no exophoric or adverbial time reference at all (with the possible exception of scientific and mathematical texts), expository texts will actually often be bound to the temporal present and telling texts to the temporal past. However, it is not the tense *per se* which denotes this, but the tense plus the additional information provided by the text itself or by the language user.

Examples from the *Corpus*:

40 how old is he
171 the first year is much brighter to my mind than the second year

In these cases the constituents of the discourse situation disambiguate the present to denote the present moment and are not of zero-quality.

3.3 It is obvious that with the two zero-tenses as axes the tense system can be organized into two groups.[4] All the other tenses DO denote temporal relations with reference to the present (as zero-tense) or the past (as zero-tense). In a present-text, the temporal past (i.e. anteriority) is denoted by the present perfect, the temporal future (i.e. posteriority) by the future. In a past-text, the temporal past (i.e. anteriority) is denoted by the past perfect, the temporal future (i.e. posteriority) by the FUTURE-IN-THE-PAST (Bull 1971).

Group of PRESENT tenses:

ZERO: He *works* at a car factory in Birmingham.
ANTE: He *has worked* at a car factory in Birmingham (for the last 20 years).
POST: (Next year), he'*ll work* at a car factory in Birmingham.

Group of PAST tenses:

ZERO: He *worked* at a car factory. (In the evenings) he *wrote* his auto-
    biography.
ANTE: He *had worked* in a car factory (for 20 years), (when the firm closed its
    doors).
POST: He said he *would work* in a car factory (if they offered him a job).

The future perfect and future-perfect-in-the-past are complex cases of POST which need not concern us here.
    Additional temporal information, as explained above, turns the ZERO-predicates into PRESENT predicates and PAST predicates respectively.
Examples (outside the *Corpus*):

PRESENT: Right now, he *works/is working* at a car factory in Birmingham.
PAST: In 1958, he *worked* at a car factory in Birmingham.

The relations of ANTE and POST remain the same. The English language does not provide for a time axis in the future with ANTE and POST relations expressed in tenses.

3.4 It is ONE task of discourse analysis to analyse tokens of texts with reference to the denotation of time as it is achieved (i) by the interplay of zero-tenses and other tenses and (ii) by the cooperation of tenses and adverbials plus exophoric reference. For this intricate task I want to offer some preliminary results arrived at by an investigation of section 1.6 of the *Corpus of Spoken English* as mentioned. This piece of discourse contains 1,235 tone groups of which, however, only 739 are taken into account. They comprise 100 per cent for the statistical comparisons that follow. The ones disregarded either do not contain finite verb forms or are planning phases (that is, immediate repetitions of utterances which were only counted once provided they contained a finite tense form), or are gambits (Edmondson and House 1981), which deserve different analytical treatment.
Tenses of sentences and clauses:

(1) present   332   44.90%
     present + modal   43   5.80%
     all others under 5% each

(2) past   227   30.70%
    all others under 5% each

Tenses and time reference in sentences and clauses:

ZERO   402   54.40%
    present   315   42.60%
    present + modal   42   5.80%
    all others under 5% each

PAST   243   32.90%
    past   204   27.90%
    all others under 5% each

This obviously is present-text interspersed with past-passages. The communicative functions which one understands in reading coincide with the statistical distribution of predicates (Figure 3.1).
Additional references to time:

adverbs (A)   78   10.50% (66.70% from 117)
prepositional phrases (P)   23   3.10% (19.70% from 117)
clauses (C)   16   2.10% (13.60% from 117)
APC   117
61 APC (= 52.10% from 117) go with past-forms
19 APC (= 16.20% from 117) go with present and present + modal forms
18 APC (= 15.40% from 117) go with present perfect and present
perfect + modal forms
all others under 5% each
444 forms of the present-group have 45 (= 10.10%) additional APC
                                                       (= 6.20% from 739)
288 forms of the past-group have 72 (= 25.00%) from additional APC
                                                       (= 9.70% from 739)

It is interesting to see from the percentage scores that only every tenth predicate in the present-group has an additional time reference, whereas it is every fourth predicate of the past-group. This means, with reference to this one text, but not refuted by others so far, that past-passages within a present-text show a strong statistical tendency to be linked to a concrete time reference. It is much stronger than temporal specification in the present-passages.

This tendency is underlined if we compare the occurence of APC not with tense forms, but with time reference.

62 APC (= 52.90% from 117) go with PAST reference
15 APC (= 13.70% from 117) go with ZERO reference
12 APC (= 10.30% from 117) go with PRESENT reference
 9 APC (= 7.70% from 117) go with RECENT PAST reference[5]

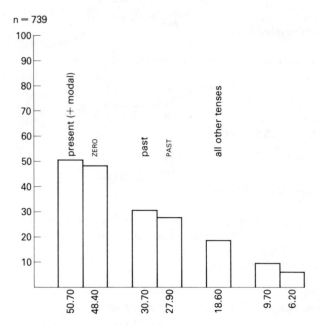

Figure 3.1

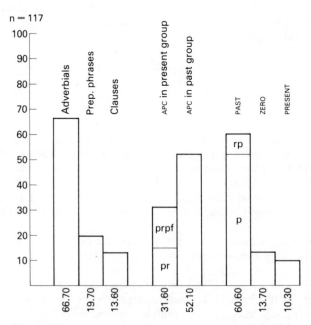

Figure 3.2

The percentage scores mean that 60.60 per cent of (recent) past reference is achieved with the help of additional temporal information—that is, more than every second token— and only 10.30 per cent of present reference—that is, every tenth token (Figure 3.2).

This is again stressed by the observation that, semantically, many adverbials cover more than one predicate or one sentence. Roughly speaking, every 2.5 adverbial does this. And by far the most of these belong to predicates of the past-group (Table 3.1). It is obvious that such statistical analyses provide only a superficial knowledge of the linguistic means which denote time in a text; they can still lead to an overview of how these means are distributed and function together. The occurrence of zero-tenses and other tenses plus adverbials is a particularly interesting point. It goes without saying that a statistical analysis like this has to be matched with a pragmatic analysis of the text within its context.

Table 3.1 Range of APC

	numbers of tone units	numbers of sentences	numbers of tokens
last week	2	3	2
before last	3	2	5
afterwards	5	4	2
some years later	6	6	4
when he was 20	7	8	1
a week ago	8	5	2
one Saturday morning	9	9	2
now	10	6	3
in 1960	13	8	1
once	16	11	1
when I was at school	18	7	1
now	22	16	2
temporarily	27	14	1
about 10 years ago	43	14	1
once	50	32	1

29 APC out of 117 (= 24.70%) cover more than 1 tone unit/sentence.
25 APC (from 29) with a coverage of 290 tone untis occur in *past*-sentences.
 4 APC (from 29) with a coverage of 45 tone units occur in *present*-sentences.

This is also true for an analysis of which adverbials go with which tense and with which time reference:

Present and present + modal:
ZERO: never, then, often, always, immediately, already
PRESENT: now, today, at lunch time

FUTURE: next year
Present continuous:
ZERO: always
PRESENT: now still
Present perfect:
ZERO: ever
PRESENT: now
REC. PAST: just, recently, this term, lately
PAST: a couple of months ago
LOOK BACK:[6]   often, ever, all these years, so late
Future:
ZERO: ever
going to:
FUTURE: any longer
Past:
REC. PAST: now, finally
PAST: never, then, always, once, every, still, before, this morning, immediately, one day, any longer, last . . ., a couple of years, afterwards, eventually, some years later
Past continuous:
PAST: immediately before, one Saturday morning
Past perfect:
PRE-PAST: then
PAST: temporarily
LOOK BACK: always
Future perfect + modal:
ZERO: any time

3.5 There are two obvious exceptions to PRESENT and PAST in their definition as zero-tenses. One is the usage of the so-called HISTORICAL PRESENT, and the usage of the PAST in polite language, for example, in an utterance like 'I wanted to ask you for support in this matter', meaning 'I want to ask . . .'. They do not, however, refute the system. On the contrary, they confirm that the tenses, used in this way, do not carry a temporal meaning, but a psychological one. This use of the zero-tenses has been called METAPHORICAL. In the HISTORICAL PRESENT a report is given AS IF it were a statement. The psychological directness of the present-text takes the place of the psychological indirectness of the past-text and gives it extra actuality and drama. In very much the same way, a statement is given AS IF it were a report in the utterance mentioned above. The psychological indirectness of the past-text here takes the place of the psychological directness of the present-text and thus makes it more tentative and polite. Metaphorical usage of PRESENT and PAST actually confirms their zero-status. There is no example of this in the discourse analysed.

The other exception is the isolated past-utterance in a present-text. There is no example in the analysed discourse, but a fabricated example might run like this: 'What you said is simply not true. I didn't call you a liar, but suggested

that you have no proof for your assumptions. And I still am of this opinion.'
Here the past clearly has no zero-function but a temporal meaning. This
meaning obviously is provided by the contrast between the one utterance with
the past-predicate and the surrounding utterances with present-predicates.
Such inserted passages mostly refer to the recent past and link up with the
preceding discourse.

In this case, the test as a whole provides the clue that a past-form is to be
understood as a concrete time reference.[7] This refers back to the point of
departure of my investigation: the denotation of time is achieved by the entire
discourse and not by the tenses *per se*.

NOTES

1. See also Émile Benveniste 1972 (*Problèmes de linguistique générale*, Paris; Gallimard,
   Chapter 19) for a similar way of analysing the French tense system.
2. The numbers are those given to the tone units in the *Corpus*. All examples are from
   section 1.6. The utterances are quoted without the intonational and prosodic
   marking.
3. Questions of aspect, though applying, will not be considered. However, a warning is
   raised against the common opinion that the PRESENT CONTINUOUS always denotes
   something going on at the moment of encoding.
   Example from the *Corpus*:

   66 he's working for a Ph.D.

   Here the predicate clearly covers the past and the present.
4. This proves that my hypothesis provides a new rationale to an old insight.
5. The RECENT PAST refers to preceding parts of the discourse. See below.
6. LOOK BACK denotes a limitless past, seen from the present.
7. In this paper I cannot investigate the influence of person on tenses. Note that first
   and second person tend to go together with temporal denotation of tenses, whereas
   third person tends to go together with zero-tenses ('I told you to wash that car' vs.
   'He told his brother to wash that car').

4 Cognitive verbs and the indication of utterance function

University of Aarhus, Denmark

4.1 INTRODUCTION

Initially, I would like to make my position clear with regard to certain points of theory and terminology. The two schools of thought that I have found most inspiring in my work with discourse analysis are speech act theory, as initiated by Austin, and ethnomethodological analysis, as developed by Sacks, Jefferson and Schegloff. As will no doubt be apparent, my approach is strongly influenced by these authors, though I hope to be able to show some further development, and in particular some integration of these theories.

Terminologically, however, I shall deviate somewhat. Rather than trying to define and use terms like 'speech act' and 'illocutionary force' (there are already quite a number of definitions on the market), I shall take as one of my basic terms 'utterance function', defined as follows.

'Utterance' is whatever is said, and 'an utterance' is a sequence of speech by one speaker, with pauses or other speakers around it. (It is possible to be more specific than that (cf. Arndt forthcoming), but for the present it will suffice.)

'Function' may seem equally straightforward, perhaps deceptively so. There are at least three meanings of the word which should be initially recognized:

F_1: the function of x = what x is used for
F_2: the function of x = what x is designed to be used for
F_3: the function of x to y = the relationship of x to y

Thus a very frequent F_1 of a paperweight is that of murder weapon, as any reader of crime fiction will know, yet we would hesitate to call that the F_2 of a paperweight. F_3 is exemplified in syntax where, say, an 'object' is the function of a nominal to a transitive verb.

Now the metaphor of 'tool' for 'utterance', implied above has its limitations. In particular, utterances are instantly produced and infinitely formally variable in a way that tools are not. And since there is no one-to-one correspondence between form and function in language, F_2 would seem to be controversial. In the following I shall assume that it is possible in principle to assign to an utterance an F_1 (i.e. how it is used) and/or an F_3 (i.e. what is its relationship to another utterance). As for F_2, I shall assume that utterances can contain certain signals which indicate what the utterance is designed to be used for, and which help the interpretation. However, I shall NOT assume that the F_2 indicated by certain such 'functional indicators' (FIs) is always identical with the actual function (F_1 or F_3) of the utterance in which they occur. The presence (or absence) of FIs is not conclusive of the interpretation, only indicative. And finally, we cannot at all assume that a particular form, once identified as an FI, will always indicate the same function, nor even that it will always be an FI. I believe we have reached a point where exemplification is imperative.

(1) I promise to come at three.
(2) I promise you there was nobody there.
(3) I promise only when I am sure I can keep my promises.
(4) A: Can I count on you two to come then?
(5) B: Yes. I'll be there.
(6) C: Yea but I have some work to do.

In (1) *I promise* is an FI of the F_1 'promising' (cf. Austin's 'explicit performative', 1962: 69ff.). Also in (2) *I promise* is an FI, though not of 'promising', but of, say, 'assuring'. In (3) *I promise* is not an FI, and the function of the utterance is difficult to assess out of context. In (5) B responds positively to (4), and this positive response (an F_3) is indicated by the FI *yes*; (5) further counts as a promise, but this F_1 is not explicitly indicated, it is interpretable from context only. (I shall return to the difference between F_1 and F_3.) (6) is a contradictive response (or at least 'qualified support') to (4), and this negative response (an F_3) is indicated by the FI *yea but*.

It will be clear that FIs provide only part of the basis for the interpretation of utterance function. The main part is context, including our knowledge about the propositional content of the utterance, and even context can be inconclusive, in that utterance function can be ambiguous. With this note of warning and vagueness we can go on to a consideration of cognitive verbs as functional indicators.

4.2 'CAUTIOUS STATEMENTS'

We all know how useful is the phrase *I think* in conversation, perhaps particularly in academic and intellectual conversation, to suggest a certain caution or reserve in a statement. It is not very common outside unrehearsed spoken language (and fiction purporting to be such). The following example is from an interview with Brzezinski:

(7) Question: What will Andropov's priorities be?
    Answer: I ASSUME that Andropov is going to persist in squelching all
              political opposition. But MY GUESS IS that he will try to combine
              that with what might be called a rationalization of the Soviet

economic system: no drastic decentralization but an effort to
get rid of the bottlenecks, to stimulate more innovation, to
introduce more modern techniques for the management of an
almost chaotically corrupt and inefficient system.

Question: Do you expect Andropov to make early gestures of conciliation
towards the West, or will he assert his tough-guy side?

Answer: I THINK it depends very much on what we do. I THINK we are in
a position to try to move him in one direction or to push him in
another. This is why, in spite of my reputation as a hawk, I
FEEL it's a good time to be forthcoming. [Newsweek,
November 22, 1982, p. 19, my emphasis]

Note, first, that not only I THINK but all the phrases I have emphasized strike
the same note of 'caution', and that formally they all share the presence of a
first person pronoun and a verb of cognition (even though GUESS is nominal-
ized). Secondly, Brzezinski is here speculating about the character and
intentions of a newly elected world leader, which is a good reason to be
cautious. This means that if we assume that there is such a function as
'cautious statement', and that Brzezinski is here using language in that
function, with I THINK and the other phrases as FIs, then this interpretation is
borne out by contextual knowledge.

I want to argue that I THINK, and the other phrases, are in fact FIs, but that
'cautious statement' is not the best term for the corresponding function
because a basic classification suggests other terms.

4.3 SOME FUNCTIONAL INDICATORS

Lyons (1977: 805) suggest that the following correspondences are similar:

(8) I will come. : I PROMISE to come.
(9) It may be raining. : I THINK it's raining.
(10) Is it raining? : I WONDER whether it's raining.
(11) It's raining : I TELL you it is raining.

Obviously only I PROMISE (8) and I TELL (11) conform to Austin's 'hereby' test.
But then explicit performatives are only one type of FI, even if perhaps a very
clear one. Others are, for instance the addition *and that's a promise*, or sentence
structure like the interrogative and declarative structures of (10) and (11), or
modal verbs like *may* in (9), or intonation patterns. Given this formal
variation, how do we recognize FIs? Well, as language users we are fairly
competent at it; as an analyst I have not reached the point where I can
confidently put forward a more exact definition than the one implied here: a
lexical, structural, or intonational configuration which helps me to interpret
and understand what an utterance does, or is meant to do, in social
interaction.

4.4 TWO WAYS OF 'THINKING'

However, one way of obtaining a more reliable distinction between what is an FI and what is not is to speculate on the classification and inventory of utterance functions. For if we know what types of functions to look for, it will be easier to identify the FIs that help us to recognize them. The function corresponding to the FI of caution exemplified in (7) is not accommodated very well in the system I am going to propose, mainly because it seems that the ubiquitous *I think* indicates two superficially similar, but in fact quite distinct functions. Consider:

(12) I think he's a fool.
(13) I think he's a carpenter.

It is fairly obvious, I believe, that the interpretation of *I think* is different in (12) and (13). The difference may become evident if we add the exclamation *Christ* in front of either: in (12) this would add conviction and strength to my negative evaluation of him, whereas in (13) it would add the element of surprise—apart from the fact that it is much less likely to occur in front of (13). By way of glossing I suggest that (12) and (13) correspond to (14) and (15) respectively:

(14) In my opinion he's a fool.
(15) I assume he's a carpenter.

And by way of explanation I suggest that *I think* of (12) indicates that this is an expression of a personal attitude, whereas the *I think* of (13) indicates that the speaker has insufficient evidence to assert as a fact that *he is a carpenter*. Common to both is the element of caution: the speaker introduces into the utterance his personal involvement either as 'giver of opinion' or as 'assessor of facts'. Note that the removal of *I think* changes very little in the communicative potential of (12), whereas in (13) it changes the meaning from non-factive to factive.

As further evidence of the naturalness of the distinction between 'expressives' like (12) and (14) and 'assumptives' like (13) and (15), let me briefly show how English compares with Danish and German in this respect:

	English	Danish	German
Assumptive	I think/assume	jeg tror	ich glaube
Expressive	I think/in my opinion	jeg synes	ich finde

Other phrases could be found in all three languages to indicate both assumptives and expressives. But the point is that of the three languages only English has the option of a common FI. A Dane, at least, translating from English into Danish will make his choice between *tror* and *synes* without hesitation. It is the ease with which the distinction is made which convinces me of its justification, and suggests its universality. It is the same ease with which an English speaker recognized that (14) and (15), respectively, are natural replacements for (12) and (13), whereas (16) and especially (17) are not:

(16) I assume he's a fool.
(17) In my opinion he's a carpenter.

4.5 A SYSTEM OF REFERENTIAL FUNCTIONS

By way of summarizing, let me tabularize the terms in the system proposed:

(18) Main categories   Subtypes   Examples
     representative   reportive   He is a carpenter.
                           assumptive   I think he is a carpenter.
     expressives   I think he is a fool.

To which should be added:

(19) regulative   commissive   I promise to come.
                          directive   I order you to go.
                          institutive   I pronounce you man and wife.

I shall refer to these together as 'referential functions'. Reportives and assumptives are subsumed under the same main category because assumptives do the same as reportives, i.e. refer to facts, only without conviction. Expressives refer to feelings, opinions or attitudes; regulatives refer to acts to be performed (these definitions are crude and provisional, but brief).

Regulatives have been very prominent in speech act investigations (cf. e.g. Searle), and I shall not concern myself with them here, apart from a remark on subdivision: the criterion used is agency. Commissives establish an agency obligation of the speaker; directives attempt to establish one for the addressee, and institutives establish a state of affairs by which anybody concerned will have to abide. Agency obligation is, however, often indeterminate, as for instance in invitations; and the appointment of, say, a sentry both directs and institutes (cf. the implications of the utterance *I am only acting under orders*). Also expressives can be subdivided; however, in the following I shall focus mainly on representatives.

The main categories notwithstanding, the ubiquity and ambiguity of *I think* suggests that at least in English the distinction between reportives and the other types is felt to be a basic one. More universally, the same thing is suggested by the implication of (18) and (19): that 'reportive' is the only category for which an FI does not spring easily to mind—it is the 'unmarked' term of the system. This is all the more salient since assumptives can have many different FIs; to mention but a few: *I believe/assume/suppose/gather/guess/ imagine/wonder/doubt* (as well as others that contain no cognitive verbs). Incidentally, the list suggests that they vary in strength of conviction, that they are spread unevenly on a scale from factive to counterfactive. But though the distiction between reportives and the other types is systematically an unmarked–marked distinction, assumptives may occur without, and reportives with, an FI.

On the one hand, assumptives can be indicated only contextually; as noted above, my contextual knowledge would allow me to interpret (7) as chiefly assumptive, even if the FIs had been left out. This point has educational implications. In my own teaching I have found that attention to the distinction between reportives, assumptives, and value-indicating expressives (which I call a RAVE-analysis—education thrives on catchy terms), as well as to the presence or absence of FIs, enables students to attain a better understanding of the function of, for instance, newspaper texts: what a mass communication text does to its reader in the way of report or comment.

Reportives, on the other hand, can be indicated, and one way of doing it is the one suggested by Lyons (cf. (11) above). Among cognitive verbs, the reportive indicator is *I know*. But if reportives are naturally unmarked, when or why do we use FIs with them?

4.6 INTERACTIONAL FUNCTIONS

A consideration of what circumstances may lead speakers to use a reportive FI gives rise to a consideration of why the system proposed in (18) and (19) is, though categorically exhaustive, nevertheless insufficient. Consider:

(20) A: John hasn't done it.
(21) B: No, I suppose he hasn't.
(22) A: I know he hasn't.

Apart from the purely formal difference of ellipsis, (20) and (22) are the same. There is no reason to believe that (22) is, or is meant to be, more factive than (20). The only difference is apparently their place in the interaction. It seems then that in order to account for the function indicated by *I know* in (22), we have to determine it along more than one functional dimension. Apart from the referential dimension, (22) is also determinable along an interactional functional dimension. (22) is a particular type of response, that is, 'reaffirming', which is defined by its place in a particular pattern of interaction, roughly describable as 'affirming–doubting–reaffirming'.

Where the referential function is the F_1 type, the interactional function is the F_3 one. The terms of the latter, which are largely those that have occupied ethnomethodologists, should include terms for the structural elements of the encounter as a whole, and of exchanges within the encounter (Arndt forthcoming). However, for the present discussion the most significant are the lowest-level ones: elicitatives and responsives, defined in terms of the mutual relationships between utterances. Elicitatives can be further differentiated in terms of the type of response they call for, responsives according partly to whether they are positive or negative (supportive or contradictive), partly according to the referential function of the exchange in which they occur. Note that 'elicitative'and 'responsive' are general terms for the components of any 'adjacency pair' (Schegloff and Sacks 1974 238 ff.).

I have found that operating with referential and interactional functions as distinct, though interrelated dimensions clears up a number of otherwise obscure points in functional or 'speech act' linguistics, as I hope to be able to demonstrate. But problems are like fairy-tale dragon heads: one solved means others cropping up.

4.7 THE TYPE–TOKEN DISTINCTION

What is the difference between the determination of the referential F_1 by context (cf. above section 4.1 and 4.2) and the relational definition of the interaction F_3?

A consideration of the type–token distinction will clarify the issue. We define a type of function; we determine an instance as a token of that type. Referential functions are defined in terms of reference (to fact, act, or opinion, cf. section 4.5). Interactional functions are defined in terms of mutual relation (e.g. elicitation–response), that is placement in interactional structure. The determination of both referential and interactional functions is based on explicit FIs and on contextual knowledge (: the sum of specific and general background knowledge that can be brought to bear on the interpretation).

For further justification of the distinction between dimensions, note that the terms along the referential dimension may be used to describe the 'macro'-function of units above the utterance: an exchange or a whole encounter. Not so the interactional terms: unlike, say, 'representative', 'responsive' cannot naturally describe a whole dialogue.

4.8 THE RELATION BETWEEN REFERENTIAL AND INTERACTIONAL FUNCTIONS

Considering that we will generally be able to assign both types of function to an utterance, what is the relation between them?

Consider the following description of (20)–(22):

(23)		ref. function	interact. function	prop. cont.
	(20)	reportive	—	—
	(21)	assumptive	response to (20)	identical with (20)
	(22)	reportive	response to (21)	identical with (21)

This description perhaps does not contain all the functional information that competent speakers can derive from the exchange. But it does capture some salient features: (21) is a contradictive response of the type I have called 'doubting' by virtue of the fact that it repeats the content of the preceding utterance, explicitly changing the referential function to assumptive. And (22) is a response of the type 'reaffirming' because, again with propositional content identical, it explicitly changes back to reportive. In other words, the use of terms defined in more than one dimension enables us to determine utterance function in actual discourse more accurately than in a unidimensional system. Similarly, the well-known 'speech act' of 'promising' can be described as one out of two possible supportive response types to a 'directive': either you comply immediately, most often to the accompaniment of a verbal acceptance, or you accept without immediate compliance. The former could be called 'assenting', the latter 'promising'. Incidentally, I find that this basically responsive character of 'promising' has often been overlooked.

4.9 WHY NOT THREE DIMENSIONS?

Actually, I believe we can profitably introduce one more functional dimension, of the F_3 type, only in this case the relation is not utterance-to-utterance, but proposition-to-proposition. Let us call this content coherence: the function of the propositional content of one (part of an) utterance relative to the propositional content of another (part of an) utterance. Roughly, the terms along the content coherence functional dimension would seem to include:

(24) (a) Symmetrical: Identity (repetition/reformulation)
                            Negation
                            (Incompatible) alternative
                            Temporal simultaneity
                            Contrast
    (b) Complementary: Spatial (left:right, above:below, etc.)
                            Temporal sequence (before:after)
                            Substantiation:conclusion
                            Reason:consequence
                            Exemplification/specification:generalization

Identity has already been illustrated in (23). Consider further:

(25) A: Can I count on you to come then?
(26) B: Yea but I have some work to do.
(27) A: I understand I can't count on you.

Everyday language, which records what we understand about functions as about anything else, has three different ways of rendering (27) in 'loose' indirect speech: A *expressed* his displeasure with B (in that the phrase *can't count on you* has negative overtones of unreliability); A *responded* rather brusquely to B (: contradictively, in that A chooses to focus on B's refusal, rather than accepting B's excuse); and A concluded that he could not count on B (he has to conclude—though he need not have done it verbally—in that B in (26) does not directly negate the proposition of (25), but softens his refusal by way of 'reporting' an 'incompatible alternative'). Note that the macro-function of this short exchange is 'directive', even though only (25) in itself is: again, in 'loose' indirect speech the whole exchange could have been rendered as 'A tried to get B to come but failed'. Note further that if A had wanted to give a supportive response, this could naturally have taken the form of 'minimal response', for example:

(27a) A: Oh I see.

Minimal responses are peculiar in being determinable only along the interactional dimension: since they neither represent, nor regulate, nor express any propositional content, they can have no referential or content coherence function. Note finally that *I understand* in (27) is an FI of 'conclusion': it usually also suggests 'assumptive'. Alternative FIs are *I gather*, *I take it*, or *so*.

Finally, polite refusals yield an interesting illustration of the interplay of the dimensions. They are commonly formulated as 'apologies' and/or 'excuses':

(28) A: Could you please tell me the way to the station?
(29) B_1: I'm afraid not.
(30) B_2: I'm a stranger here myself.

Both (29) and (30) are contradictive responses to (28). (29) referentially 'expresses' regret and provides an explicit 'negation' of the content of (28). This configuration describes the type of 'apology' that can be used to refuse a request, and *I'm afraid* can be considered an FI of this function. On the other hand, (30) 'reports' a proposition which constitutes a 'reason' for an implied 'negation' of (28). This configuration (together with the one suggested for (26)) describes this type of 'excuse': common to (26) and (30) is 'reportive' and 'implied negation'. Note that 'apology' and 'excuse' are very commonly combined, simply by the insertion of the FI *I'm afraid* in front of the excuse.

The possibility of 'implied' content coherence relates the present discussion to Grice's notion of 'implicature' (Grice 1975), in particular, the 'maxim of relevance'.

4.10 EXPLOITATION

The exploration of the three-dimensional functional description could be continued in further detail. But I believe the theory has been fully enough expounded for me to be able to take up a more interesting strain: the exploitation of functions and FIs in everyday speech. For it seems to me that our expertise in handling these is such that we are able not only to use them, but also to exploit them: in fact in some cases to abuse them so as to add, consciously or subconsciously, extra layers of meaning.

The text extracts below have been taken from fiction. I would have liked to illustrate equally from non-fiction. However, the major consideration has been illustrative potential. Anyway, the authors show a skill with dialogue which I find convincing, and my experience with natural conversation assures me that the analysis covers many aspects of non-fictive dialogue as well.

(31) (Six parachutists, some of them inexperienced, are making ready to jump over the Alps. One, the radio operator, has put on his snow-smock.)
   ... He turned round questioningly as a hand tapped the hummocked outline below his white smock.
3   —'I hardly like to say this,' Schaffer said diffidently, 'but I really don't reckon your radio is going to stand the shock of landing, Sergeant.'
   —'Why not?' Harrod looked more lugubrious than ever. 'It's been done
6   before.'
   —'Not by you, it hasn't. By my reckoning you're going to hit the ground with a terminal velocity of a hundred and eighty miles an hour. Not to
9   put too fine a point on it, I think you're going to experience some difficulty in opening your chute.'
   —Harrod looked at him, looked at his other five smockless companions,
12   then nodded slowly and touched his own smock. 'You mean I put this on AFTER we reach the ground?'
   —'Well,' Schaffer said consideringly, 'I really think it would help.' He
15   grinned at Harrod, who grinned back almost cheerfully. Even Carra-ciola's lips twitched in the beginnings of a smile. The release of tension within that frozen fuselage was almost palpable.
[Alistair Maclean, *Where Eagles Dare*, Fontana, 1969, p. 16]

The main point here is the use for humourous effect of the assumptive FIs *I reckon* (line 4), *by my reckoning* (7), *I think* (9), *I really think* (14). Though predictions, Schaffer's propositions leave no room for doubt, caution or assumption; if you wear a smock over your parachute, you are most definitely going to experience a fatal landing. So, as far as everyday language is concerned, Descartes was wrong—there are propositions you can be sure of, and if you pretend to doubt them, the effect will naturally be that of humour or ridicule. Obviously, Schaffer's humour manifests itself in other ways as well, but the exploitation of the FIs is definitely part of it. As a minor point we may note that the negation in line 4 is a displaced one: if it had not been, the phrase would, in all likelihood, not have been an FI.

In the following extract, where two people discuss their daughter's education, the use and exploitation of functions is somewhat more complex.

(32) —'... I don't know what I think about it,' said Mor. ...
   —'Well, I know what I think about it,' said Nan. 'Our finances and her
3   talents don't leave us much choice, do they?'
   —'I suggest we wait a while,' said Mor. 'Felicity doesn't know her own mind yet.' ...
6   —'You always pretend people don't know what they want when they don't want what you want,' said Nan. ... 'You must take some

responsibility for the children. I know you have all sorts of fantasies about yourself. But at least try to be realistic about THEM.'

9 —Mor winced. . . . He made an effort. 'You may be right,' he said, 'but I still think we ought to wait.'

—'I know I'm right,' said Nan. . . .

12 —He tried to change the subject. 'I wonder if Felicity will mind your having changed her room around?'

[Iris Murdoch, *The Sandcastle*, Penguin, 1960, pp. 12–13.]

As minor points we may note that the *I know* followed by a wh-clause (lines 1 and 2) is not an FI, or at least not the same FI as the *I know* followed by a that-clause. Nor is the negation in line 1 a displaced one. And of course the use of *know* with other subjects than the 1st person does not constitute an FI (e.g. lines 4 and 6). The same holds for the *I think* which is not followed by a that-clause (lines 1 and 2).

More interesting is the exploitation of *I know* in lines 8 and 12. Line 12 is clearly reminiscent of (22) above: Nan reaffirms her position (affirmed earlier: that Felicity should join a secretarial course) in response to Mor's doubt in line 10. Yet line 12 is not a reportive: it has nothing to do with representing facts, but expresses an opinion. So *I know* is exploited to add strength or conviction to an expressive. Presumably the exploitation here can be supposed to be less conscious than Schaffer's in (31).

Similarly, in line 8 *I know* is exploited to add reportive strength to a proposition that can hardly be reportive: you can only 'assume' that other people have fantasies, which they themselves may 'express'. The English language has a word for people who tend to 'report', when they can reasonably only 'assume' or 'express': the word is 'cocksure'. And I believe that the formulations of lines 8 and 12 are important elements in Iris Murdoch's description of Nan.

But the *I know* of line 8 is an FI not only for referential, but also for content coherence and interactional function. The sequence *I know . . . but* usually indicates 'ineffective reason (or substantiation) . . . reality'. In this use *I know . . . but* is synonymous with *though . . .* Consider:

(33) I know it is raining, but let's walk anyway.

(34) I know the thing floats, but it isn't cork.

(35) I know you have ambitions for yourself, but don't have the same ambitions for the children.

(36) Though you have all sorts of fantasies about yourself, at least try to be realistic about them.

In (33) the rain constitutes an—ineffective—reason not to walk. In (34) the floating—ineffectively—substantiates that it is cork. (35) is a less emotional formulation of Nan's lines 8–9: *fantasies* and *realistic* indicate her negative attitude to Mor's ambitions. (36) is, as far as I can see, synonymous with lines 8–9.

'Pre-empting contradiction' suggests itself as a term for this function: the formulation *I know ... but* indicates that the speaker is anticipating the counter-argument of a possible response and pronouncing it invalid. The elicitative force of the utterance is thus deliberately low: it elicits only agreement. A corresponding responsive use of *I know* (often elliptic) indicates a corresponding 'subempting' or 'disregarding contradiction'.

(37) Parent: Go to bed!
(38) Child: But it's only ten o'clock.
(39) Parent: I know.

(39) indicates that the speaker finds the counter-argument of (38) invalid (known, but ineffective), and (39) is practically synonymous with *Go to bed anyway* (*anyway* must be another FI of 'disregarding contradiction').

The description of Mor through his utterance functions is as significant as that of Nan. He is in retreat, as well as in doubt. Thus in line 4 he formulates a mutual regulative, with the FI *I suggest*. In line 11 he utters the same proposition, only formulated as an expressive (*I think we ought*). Obviously in the contextual interpretation the two are very nearly the same, since regulatives will normally be based on the content of an expressive, that is, an attitude or opinion. Yet considering the general gist of their conversation, it can hardly be entirely coincidental that he regresses from an explicit regulative to a more private expressive formulation.

Comparing (31) and (32), I feel justified in making a link between the functional analysis and a genre distinction. The comparatively simple and obvious exploitation of functions for irony in (31) fits in with Maclean's objective: action and humour. In contrast, the many-faceted complexities of the functional analysis of (32) reflect Murdoch's concern with psychological characterization in her dialogue.

4.11 CONCLUSION

The definition and FIs in the three-dimensional system, and the determination of functions in actual discourse on the basis of an interpretation of the interplay between FIs and contextual knowledge, are significant from the point of view of functional theory. The cognitive verbs are useful in this connection because they add a range of rather nicely differentiated signals to the inventory of FIs (besides explicit performatives, modal verbs, modal disjuncts, modal adjectives and nouns, sentence structure, etc.), thus enhancing the possibility of setting up a valid classification of functions. Moreover, cognitive verbs make an explicit link between cognition and some types of speech function, which I find significant.

However, the main point of the functional description is not the clearing up of delicacies of theory, but its practical use for educational purposes. As suggested above, a RAVE-analysis (section 4.5) can enhance students' understanding of mass communication texts; other aspects of the description, in particular the content coherence dimension (Jensen 1980), can be used for a similar purpose. Further, in my analysis of (31) and (32), I tried to indicate how the functional description could be used to substantiate both a number of observations on these two literary texts individually and the determination of a genre distinction between them.

Finally, as I have shown in more detail elsewhere (1982), I am convinced that the functional description I have given, and in particular the establishment of an inventory of FIs, will provide a useful basis for setting out a detailed functional syllabus for foreign language teaching.

5 Two ways of looking at causes and reasons

Ivan Lowe
Summer Institute of Linguistics

5.1 INTRODUCTION

This chapter[1] looks at the various kinds of causes and reasons, and the relationships between them. First, I give two different but related approaches to the problem of sorting out the various kinds of causal relationships, the approach of varying strength of causality and that of necessary versus sufficient conditions. Then I approach the problem of reasons by considering first reasons for speech acts and then establishing a relationship between reasons for speech acts and reasons for non-speech acts.

I start with the difference between causes and reasons. Consider the sentences:

(1) John got a bad shock BECAUSE he touched the high tension wire.
(2) I take my daughter by car to music lessons BECAUSE there are bad characters in that area who would harm her if she went alone.

The first is a clear case of a cause–effect relationship, where once a certain phenomenon—the cause—has been realized, the other—the effect—must follow mechanistically. The second is really quite different in that the *because*-clause gives the speaker's justification for his action in terms of his beliefs and values and here deliberation and decision are involved.

5.2 APPROACHES TO CAUSALITY

5.2.1 Scale of Causality

I present, first, two approaches to the problem of causal relationships. The first of these is that of scale of causality.[2] Consider the two sentences:

(3) If John touches the high tension wire, he will get a bad shock. (law-like causality)
(4) If John gets his visa, he will go to Brazil. (enabling causality)

Both the sentences have the surface form of a conditional (if) clause followed by a main clause. However, there is a causal relationship between the constituents of each sentence and this is different for the two sentences. In sentence (3), John's touching the h.t. wire will lead automatically and inevitably to his getting a bad shock, so there is a mechanistic law-like cause and effect relationship between the if-clause and the main clause. On the other hand, in sentence (4), getting his visa will make it possible for John to go to Brazil as without it he could not have gone, but it does not lead automatically to his going to Brazil: that is to say, even after he gets his visa John could still decide not to go. The if-clause in the second sentence expresses an ENABLING condition and this is a much weaker kind of causality than the law-like condition of sentence (3). In fact, I propose a scale of causality as illustrated by the following sentences:

(3) If John touches the high tension wire, he will get a bad shock. (law-like)
(5) If John waters his plants, they will grow. (quasi-law)
(6) If John gets his visa, he will go to Brazil. (enabling)
(7) If the weather is fine, John will go for a walk. (facilitating)

for which I say that the cause expressed by the if-clause is strongest in the first sentence (3) and gets progressively weaker in the second, third and fourth sentences ((5), (6), (7) respectively).

This scale of causality is corroborated by the different surface connectives that are permitted between the clauses for the different points along the scale. Thus the strict law-like relationship as exemplified by sentence (3) permits *so* and *because* between the constituent clauses and also allows the content of the law-like condition to be expressed in the form of a *by*—phrase. Specifically:

(3a) John touched the high tension wire *so* he got a bad shock.
(3b) John got a bad shock *because* he touched the high tension wire.
(3c) John got a bad shock *by* touching the high tension wire.

The quasi-law relationship is illustrated by sentence (5). This relationship is causally weaker than the strict law-like relationship; it is a law with a loophole, as it were. Such a sentence will still permit *so*, *because* and the *by*-phrase in just the same way as the strict law-like causal will, as can be seen by testing the sentence *If John waters his plants they will grow*. The weaker causality, however, allows us to insert hedges like *probably* or *very likely* immediately after the verb of the main clause, thus: *If John waters his plants, they will probably/very likely grow*. Such hedges cannot be used in sentences with law-like conditions, thus the following sounds strange: *If John touches the high tension wire, he'll probably get a bad shock*, when eveyone knows that the bad shock is inevitable once he has touched the wire. One would only use the last sentence sarcastically.

The enabling condition gives sentences which permit *so* between constituent clauses as in (4a) (below), and the if-then construction in this case also allows a *be able to* before the verb of the main clause as in (4aa). However, in contrast to sentences expressing the law-like conditions, we cannot use *because* as a connective or the *by*-phrase (so 4b* and 4c* are both unacceptable):

(4a) John got his visa *so* he went to Brazil.
(4aa) If John gets his visa he will *be able to* go to Brazil.
(4b*) John went to Brazil *because* he got his visa.[3]
(4c*) John went to Brazil *by* getting his visa.

5.2.2 Necessary vs. sufficient conditions[4]

A second approach to the same problem is that of necessary vs. sufficient conditions. A SUFFICIENT condition S is a condition which is of itself sufficient to realize its corresponding effect E; whereas a NECESSARY condition N is one which must be true before its corresponding effect E can possibly happen.

One must think of this approach as a different one from the previous scale of causality or else confusion will result. There are some similarities. Thus a necessary condition is very much like an enabling condition, and a sufficient condition is very much like a law-like condition. But there are also important differences, as we shall see, and we must not equate the two approaches. I treat, first, sufficient conditions and then necessary conditions.

5.2.2.1 Sufficient conditions

Two different but essential aspects of sufficiency in English can be seen by looking at the usages of BECAUSE and BY. Consider, first, the use of BECAUSE in the following three sentences:

(3b) John got a bad shock BECAUSE he touched the high tension wire.
(8)   John is in hospital BECAUSE he touched the high tension wire.
(9)   The bridge collapsed BECAUSE it had a faulty tension member.

The first sentence (3b) illustrates a SUFFICIENT condition (or sufficient cause); touching the h.t. wire was enough (or sufficient) to give John a bad shock. It also illustrates a law-like condition (or law-like cause) in that whenever someone touches the h.t. wire he gets a bad shock. Thus in this case a sufficient condition is the SAME as a law-like condition.

However, consider the second sentence (8). In the situation described there, touching h.t. wire was enough to put John in hospital so it is a sufficient condition. But on the other hand, not every one who touches an h.t. wire goes to hospital; some may be killed instantly; while others recover unscathed (but all get a shock). So here a sufficient condition is NOT the same as a law-like condition. In general, we can say that a law-like condition MUST describe a direct cause and effect relationship, whereas a sufficient CAN be direct as in the first example but it can also be indirect as in the second. Thus as a more extreme example of a sufficient condition which is indirect, we could have something like *He is in hospital* BECAUSE *he was showing off*, where the causal chain if spelled out in detail would be *He is in hospital* BECAUSE *he got a bad shock* BECAUSE *he touched the high tension wire* BECAUSE *he was showing off*. But it is clear that most of the time we do not talk this way; rather we express the relevant sufficient cause and the effect but omit the intermediate links in the causal chain.

A sufficient condition is situation-bound, whereas a law-like condition is expected to be generally true in a large variety of different situations.

Consider now the third sentence (9) in a situation where a bridge had collapsed during a recent bad storm. An engineer who knew that the bridge was originally designed and built to withstand bad storms, but who knew that the bridge had a faulty tension member, would use this sentence; for this engineer the faulty tension member was the relevant sufficient cause for the collapse rather than the storm. However, a layman without knowledge of such things would be more likely to say *The bridge collapsed because of the bad storm*, since for him it was the storm that was relevant and sufficient for the collapse. Thus relevance and observer viewpoint come into the idea of sufficiency. This is illustrated also by the all-too-common repartee between children:

A Why should I do what you told me to?
B Just BECAUSE.

Again, the idea of sufficiency and relevance is illustrated by the following uses of BY in English.

(10) He cleaned the radiator BY reverse-flushing it.
(11) John dried his clothes BY ironing them.
(12) John got the job BY bribing the personnel manager.
(13) John got malaria BY sleeping without a mosquito net.

In each of the above examples, the BY-phrase describes a means or method which was sufficient to accomplish the effect described by the main clause. Thus reverse-flushing was sufficient to clean the radiator, ironing was sufficient to dry John's clothes, bribing the personnel manager sufficient to get him the job, sleeping without a mosquito net sufficient to get him malaria. The examples differ in that the BY-phrase in the first sentence describes a standard method, in the second an unorthodox method, in the third a socially deviant method, in the fourth the means was presumably unintentional; however, in all the examples the method is sufficient or enough to bring about the effect.

5.2.2.2 *Necessary conditions*

A necessary condition N, if true, makes its corresponding effect E possible, and if N is not true then E is not possible. Thus many enabling conditions are necessary conditions. Some enabling conditions, however, are not strong enough to be necessary conditions; they merely facilitate the effects. The distinction can be seen by comparing the first two sentences of the following set with the last two.

(14) If I get my visa, I will go to Brazil. (necessary)
(15) If John comes this afternoon, I'll get him to fix the car. (necessary)
(16) If it is fine this afternoon, I'll go for a walk. (facilitative)
(17) If I get that bonus on Friday, I'll take my girl out. (facilitative)

In both the first two sentences, (14) and (15), the condition expressed in the if-clause is necessary for the effect expressed in the main clause to go through; thus specifically, without a visa I cannot go to Brazil; if John does not come, I cannot get him to fix the car. However, looking at the third and fourth sentences of the set (16) and (17), we can think of SOME situations where the if-clauses there would express facilitative conditions rather than necessary conditions. Thus being fine might make it so that I'd just find it more pleasant to go for a walk but perhaps I'd go even if it was wet. And getting that bonus might just make it that much easier for me to take my girl out, but my funds are such that I could take her out anyway, even though it would be a bit tight financially. In such situations, the last two if-clauses would express facilitative rather than enabling conditions. It is clear, though, that in other situations the same if-clauses in the same sentences could express enabling conditions; thus if I were so ill that going for a walk in the rain would be impossible, or if I were flat broke, then the if-clauses of (16) and (17) would express enabling conditions. As in the consideration of sentence (4aa), we can insert *be able to* before the main verb of the sentence when there is an enabling condition in the if-clause; however, when the if-clause expresses only a facilitating condition, *be able to* insertion is no longer acceptable.

5.3 SOME PRAGMATIC ISSUES

Clearly, any theory of causality must include an account of purpose constructions like *I went downtown in order to buy a pair of shoes*, as these are usually considered part of the causal system of a language. In order to give an account of such constructions and establish conditions for their well-formedness, I need first to digress slightly and discuss the pragmatic issues of correspondence and control. Correspondence is the matter of how many conditions correspond to how many effects, while control is the matter of whether or not the participant in focus has control over the if-clause condition or not.

5.3.1 Correspondence

How many conditions correspond to how many effects? Seldom is it a simple one-to-one correspondence.

For law-like cause and effect situations, the same effect can often be produced by difference causes as in (18) and (19).

(18) John died because he drank cyanide.
(19) John died because he had falciprum malaria.

Again, the same cause can give rise to different effects as in (20) and (21).

(20) John died because he had falciprum malaria.
(21) John suffered brain damage because he had falciprum malaria.

For enabling conditions, one-to-one, one-to-many and many-to-one correspondences are all possible between conditions and effects. Thus:

(4) If John gets his visa, he will go to Brazil. (one condition to one effect)
(22) If John goes downtown, he will buy. | a pair of shoes |
(23) | get his hair cut. | (one to many)
(24) | see a lawyer. |
(25) If John gets his car started |
(26)   his bike fixed } he'll go to Oxford. (many to one)
(27) If the buses run again today |

For sufficient conditions, there can be more than one sufficient condition for the same effect because different observers may see different conditions to be the relevant sufficient condition. Thus, to repeat a previous example:

(9)/(9a) The bridge collapsed because | it had a faulty tension member. |
                                       | it was hit by a bad storm. |

5.3.2 Control

The question here is whether the participant in focus is in control of an enabling condition or not. Thus in example (28) the participant in focus does have such control, while in (29) he does not.

(28) If I go downtown, I'll buy a pair of shoes. (+ control over enabling condition)
(29) If they sell batteries at the store, I'll get some. (− control)

5.3.3 Purpose constructions

We can now state the conditions under which an if-then sentence like

(30) If I go to the beach, I'll go for a swim.

has a well-formed agnate purpose construction like

(31) I went to the beach | in order to |
                         { so that I could } go in for a swim.
                         | because I wanted to |

The conditions are, first, the if-clause situation has to be under the control of the participant in focus—thus there is no purpose construction corresponding to *If it is fine, I'll go for a walk*, and, second, the effect has to be desirable to the participant in focus. Thus one probably would not get *John touched the high tension wire in order to get a shock* except in the case of the mentally deranged or the suicide attempt. On the other hand, one might well get *Mary ate lots in order to get fat* in a situation where Mary had previously become seriously under-weight because of some wasting disease.

Notice also that where an if-clause expresses a single enabling condition that corresponds to many effects an agnate purpose construction derived from this will select one effect and exclude the others.

Thus for (30a) which expresses one condition enabling many effects:

(30a) If I go to the beach {
I'll go for a swim.
I'll sunbathe a while.
I'll have a picnic with Jenny.

once we opt for the purpose construction, only one purpose corresponds to one enabling condition; thus:

(30b) I went to the beach in order to go for a swim.

5.4 REASONS

I pass on now from causes to reasons. We say in the introduction that reasons are to be thought of as an individual's justification for an action in terms of a set of beliefs and values (and are to be distinguished from causes which involve some cause–effect mechanism). I deal first with reasons for speech acts and then pass on to reasons for actions.

5.4.1 Reasons for speech acts

Consider the following sentences:

(32) John is home BECAUSE the lights are on.
(33) Is there a petrol station nearby BECAUSE the tank's empty?
(34) Eat it up now BECAUSE it will be no good by tomorrow.
(35) Talk to him now BECAUSE he goes to Australia tomorrow.

These four example sentences all end in *because*-clauses which give the justification for the speech act which is the main clause. The main clauses themselves express four different kinds of illocutionary acts: the first is a state-ment, the second a question, the third a request, the fourth a giving of advice. It is clear that the *because*-clauses do not give law-like or sufficient conditions under which the main clauses are true; causality in that sense is not involved here. Rather they give reasons or justifications. Thus in the first sentence, the *because*-clause justifies the statement in the main clause by giving evidence for its truth, in the second the *because*-clause justifies the asking of the question, in the third it justifies the request made, and in the fourth it justifies the advice given. All the *because*-clauses then are REASONS FOR SPEECH ACTS.

5.4.2 Reasons for actions

I pass on now to reasons for actions. Consider the following:

(36) I moved out of the house BECAUSE it was creepy there.
 (2) I take my daughter by car to music lessons BECAUSE there are bad characters in that area who would harm her if she went alone.
(37) I went to John BECAUSE he was the only one who could help us.
(38) I skipped the lecture BECAUSE I felt tired.[5]
(39) I went to the concert BECAUSE I like Bach.

In the above five sentences, the *because*-clauses do not introduce causes in any mechanistic cause–effect sense, and in every case mental processes, deliberation and choice are involved. In fact, each example could be prefixed by *I decided to* or *I wanted to*, so the first sentence, for instance, could take the form:

(36a) I decided/wanted to move out of the house because it was creepy there.

In this form, the mental process or deliberation component is very clear. We can also have:

(36b) I suggest that you move out of the house because it is creepy there.

where the main clause has the illocutionary force of a suggestion and the *because*-clause is the reason for the suggestion. Thus in both the original sentence where the main clause describes an action and the derived sentence (36b) where the first part of the sentence expresses a suggestion (for an action), the *because*-clause expresses a reason. This is then added support for the reason analysis.

5.4.3 A bridge between reasons for speech acts and reasons for actions

We can get a bridge from the reasons for speech acts, especially those for requests and advice like (34) and (35) of section 5.4.1 to reasons for actions (i.e. non-speech acts). Thus consider the following which are obviously derived from (34) and (35):

(34a) I ate it all up BECAUSE it would have been no good the day after.
(35a) I talked to him then BECAUSE he would have gone to Australia by the day after.

Imagine a situation in which someone was given one of the suggestions/advice in (34) and (35). He carries out the suggestion/advice and then later he describes what he did. The derived sentences (34a) and (35a) are then adequate descriptions of his actions and in these descriptions notice that the *because*-clauses have now become reasons for ACTIONS and not just reasons for speech acts.

At least some reasons for action then can be derived from reasons for speech acts. Can all reasons for actions be so derived? At this point it is hard to give a blanket answer to cover all cases but the answer would seem to be yes, because all reasons mean that something has been thought upon or dwelt upon and so a mental attitude is involved (as distinct from cause–effect relationships where it is not). This way of looking at the distinction between reasons and causes stems from Anscombe 1957.

5.4.3 Reasons for statements

I conclude with remarks on how reasons for statements justify the statement. Consider the following:

(32) John is home BECAUSE the lights are on.
(40) Wellington was a great general BECAUSE he beat Napoleon.
(41) The cobra is dangerous BECAUSE its bite will kill you.

The main clauses in all these sentences are statements and the *because*-clause is the speaker's justification for his statement in all cases. However, there is a difference in the way the various *because*-clauses justify. In the first sentence, the speaker is invoking a known, frequent pattern, that is, that *whenever John is at home, the lights are on*, at the moment, the lights are on so John must be at home. The speaker is making an inference on the basis of evidence checked against a known pattern and this evidence is his justification for making the statement, that he believes the statement is true. In the second and third sentences, however, the main clause is an evaluation and the *because*-clause is an appeal to commonly accepted cultural standards that the evaluation is correct; thus, specifically, anyone who can beat Napoleon must be a great general and anything that can kill you must be considered dangerous.

NOTES

1. I would like to acknowledge my intellectual debt to John Callow, David Crozier, Bob Dooley, Joe Grimes, John Sinclair and Ger Reesink who by various means from casual remarks to extended discussions, have enriched my understanding of the fascinating topic of causality.
2. The idea of a scale of causality stems, of course, from the intuition that there are strong and weak causes. This chapter justifies this linguistically.
3. In fact, the sentence *John went to Brazil because he got his visa* is an acceptable sentence under certain conditions. In the situation where John is all ready and wanting to go to Brazil and all necessary conditions (e.g. selling his house, arranging for a job in the new country, etc., etc.) have been fulfilled bar one, namely the visa, then in the event that John received his visa, the above sentence is acceptable. What has happened in this case is that when all necessary conditions bar one have been satisfied and there is a desire (or decision) to go through with the effect, then the one outstanding necessary condition becomes a sufficient condition. And, since for English *because* marks sufficient conditions as per the treatment of section 5.2.2.1,

the sentence is acceptable. This sentence, then, supports the necessary-sufficient conditions model.

4. The idea of necessary vs. sufficient conditions is discussed by philosophers; see, for example, Brandt 1975. The philosophers, however, do not back up the semantic side of their discussion with linguistic support in the form of surface structures. This I have tried to do in the present chapter.

5. It was pointed out by a discussant at Hatfield that if we rephrase (38) as *I skipped the lecture because I was* SO *tired* or as *I was* SO *tired that I skipped the lecture*, then the reason is a sufficient one. This is clearly correct since both of these rephrasings can be paraphrased by *I was tired* ENOUGH *to skip the lecture* and this last version shows the sufficiency very clearly.

Part II
Conversational strategies

The four chapters in this section—Altenberg on the ordering of causal expressions, Stenström on *really*, MacLure on adult–child talk, and Brown on discourse participants' knowledge—form a bridge between the more theoretical concerns of Part I and the wider horizons of Part III. They also show some of the ways that linguists in the 1980s are tackling spontaneous spoken language and affording speech the primacy claimed for it. All of these chapters have at their centre the analysis of some corpus of data and the investigation of some aspect of conversational structure. Altenberg and Stenström both use the same two machine-readable corpora, the *London–Lund Corpus of Spoken English* (LLC) and the *Lancaster–Oslo/Bergen Corpus of British English* (LOB), and base their conclusions on statistical as well as observational data. MacLure uses data collected for its relevance to her specific research interests, and Brown uses controlled data collection to elicit the sort of evidence she requires. Furthermore, although it is not fashionable to direct too much attention to the methodology of linguistics, the various research methods used are themselves not the least interesting aspect of these chapters.

The first chapter in the section, by Bengt Altenberg, provides an interesting link with Lowe, the final contributor to the last section. Like Lowe, he is also interested in causality but take his evidence about van Dijk's four types of causal ordering—NATURAL, COGNITIVE, THEMATIC and PRAGMATIC—from naturally occurring texts. It is particularly interesting to contrast Altenberg's statistical study of contextualized passages from two 100,000-word corpora with Lowe's detailed discussion of sentences constructed to fill places in an acceptability pattern. The latter approach allowed the exhaustive pursuit of a particular theme, while the former always throws up more data and attendant difficulties than you bargained for. The juxtaposition of both approaches to aspects of the same problem demonstrates each method's own unique contribution to linguistics.

Nevertheless, each approach has its own dangers and certain points must be borne in mind from the start. In the case of corpus work it is important to remember what we are working with and its relationship to the subject of our research. The LOB corpus is made up of public informative prose and the LLC sample consists of transcriptions of spoken English. At first glance, my formulation here may seem unnecessarily roundabout but it becomes important in several contexts. It is my belief that prose—a written category—is a primary datum for linguistic study side by side with speech. Transcriptions are not data but tools.

The distinction is useful, for instance, when we want to count type-token ratios. Altenberg has discovered that in the LLC sample *because* and *so* make up 80 per cent of all the causal connectors, while the six most common written connectors (*because*, *for*, *therefore*, *since*, *thus* and *so*) make up only 62 per cent of the LOB corpus. This is obviously an important discovery and Altenberg rightly draws attention to the possibilities available to the writer to concentrate on stylistic elegance, because he is not subject to the same real-time constraints as the speaker is.

There is, however, an important point deriving from the distinction between prose and transcription. Part of the reason why the writer has to use visually different tokens—which are classified in the grammar book and dictionary as different words—derives from the loss of the phonological possibilities allowed by speech to differentiate between levels of such notions as connectedness and disjunction. This is a particular case of the general truth that the graphic mode—especially print—is discrete and all-or-none, while the phonic mode is subject to fine modulations of more-or-less. Not every token, therefore, that we are forced to write with the graphic sequence *because* is presented to the decoder in the same way in the spoken language. As a result, one of the hardest lessons facing the child learning to write prose is that written language has to signal purely lexicogrammatically what speech can signal phonologically as well. This at least partly explains why speech is often said to be paratactic and writing hypotactic. In fact, given the rich possibilities of speech, you can signal all sorts and degrees of subordination and connection without having to encode it all in the lexicogrammar. So because only two items as transcribed make up 80 per cent of all the causal connectors in the spoken corpus, it does not follow that all these tokens are phonologically the same and still less that they represent only two underlying items as they would in writing. The statistical point is still valid and interesting, but the detailed analysis of the sound recordings of the data will reveal even more.

This point is well illustrated by Stenström in her investigation of *really* in the same two data bases. She shows that this written token is in fact used to represent five separate items, which she calls after their functions, INTENSIFIER, EVALUATER, PLANNER, REOPENER and CONTINUER. Like Altenberg's causal connectors, *really* is much more common in conversation transcripts than in written texts and certain types are practically exclusive to conversations. These are the ones associated with the turn-taking system and characteristically occurring in a tone group all to themselves. Stenström's detailed analysis of the grammar of her transcribed material side by side with its prosodic features clearly illustrates the significance of position and pronunciation alongside lexicogrammatical items in signalling text structure.

Even the single tone group uses of *really* are internally diverse. On the one hand, there are examples where the item carries very little lexicogrammatical meaning and is probably best compared with alexical tone-carriers like *mhmh*. Even in these cases, however, there is still some element of meaning derived from the use of this particular word. Sometimes there are echoes of the meaning of *truly*, sometimes the use of the word is characteristic of the speaker, correlates with their age or sex, or with certain speech styles more than others. At the other extreme, it is one of the signals of the hypothetical–real relation discussed in Winter 1977.

Both Stenström and Altenberg emphasize the importance of position in discourse. Altenberg states that, of the four basic principles of ordering mentioned above—NATURAL, COGNITIVE, THEMATIC and PRAGMATIC—the pragmatic principle is by far the most important in determining the ordering of causally related clauses. In other words, the encoder follows the speech act sequence or the development of the discourse topic. In a most perceptive analysis of the structuring of spontaneous conversation, he goes on to show how topic development works more at a local, rather than a global level in speech.

While the previous contributors discussed aspects of 'normal' conversation, MacLure throws light on the normal by discussing special cases. She looks at the kind of strategies used by adults to children who have not yet learned conversational skills to allow a pseudo-interaction and at the same time to provide a foothold in communicative behaviour through this proto-conversation. These strategies provide an insight into the meanings inherent, as it were, in the language, aside from the intentions of the interactants and they parallel the kind of methods all of us use in the case of conversational breakdown and difficulty. Constraints like non-repeatability of first elements in a pair have also to be learned.

Finally in this section we have another illustration that different methodologies have their own values in understanding language. While Altenberg and Stenström used machine-readable corpora, and MacLure based her work on the analysis of a specific type of interaction she had collected, Brown uses controlled data elicitation to achieve her objects. Her focus of interest is how interactants package their information differently in terms of different perceived knowledge states in their interlocutor. This is familiar in the different responses we all make to questions such as *Where are you from?* The way we encode the answer will depend among other things on whether we think it is a question of our birthplace or our present abode, and on how well we think our interlocutor knows the area, etc. In Brown's experiment she gives all the information to the experimental subjects except that, while she knows what the individual subjects know, they have to establish where they differ from each other in terms of information. And they react to this by using definite and indefinite expressions, subtly modulated as their perceptions change.

6 Causal ordering strategies in English conversation

Bengt Altenberg

Lund University, Sweden

6.1 INTRODUCTION

The expression of causal relations is a rewarding area for anyone interested in discourse structure. There are several reasons for this. Causal relations play an important role in human communication and are frequently expressed in most types of speech and writing. They appear in a variety of lexical and grammatical forms whose use and appropriateness are determined by various contextual factors. What is of special significance for an exploration of discourse structure is that many cause–result expressions permit a transposition of the related propositions without a subsequent change of (cognitive) meaning, as in the following examples (taken from van Dijk 1977: 206 f.):

(1) (a) Peter had an accident, so he is in hospital.
    (b) Because he had an accident, Peter is in hospital.
    (c) Peter is in hospital, because he had an accident.

These examples express the same relation between a cause C and a result R, but in (1a) and (1b) the cause is presented before the result (yielding what I shall call 'CR order'), whereas in (1c) the sequence is reversed (resulting in 'RC order'). However, the difference is not merely one of linear order. In (1a) the two propositions are encoded at the same syntactic level and linked by a conjunct (parataxis); in (1b) and (1c) they are expressed at different syntactic levels and linked by a subordinator (hypotaxis).

As has been pointed out in several studies (e.g. Halliday and Hasan 1976; van Dijk 1977; Winter 1982), the choice between causal variants of this kind is largely a matter of contextual perspective, such as thematic structure and topic development in discourse. However, these factors are also dependent on the different planning conditions inherent in different types of discourse. It is this latter aspect that will be emphasized in this chapter.

The strong dependence of causal expression on the situational aspects of discourse was revealed to me in a recent statistical study of causal connecters that I made within the framework of the research project 'English in Speech and Writing' at Lund University (see Altenberg 1984; on the project see also Tottie *et al.* 1983). The material used for this study consisted of a 100,000-word sample of surreptitiously recorded conversation from the *London–Lund Corpus of Spoken English* (published in Svartvik and Quirk 1980: 14 ff.) and an equal amount of public informative prose from the *Lancaster–Oslo/Bergen Corpus of British English* (described in Johansson *et al.* 1978; Hofland and Johansson 1982). The investigation included a range of connective types, such as conjunctions (*because*, *as*, *since*, etc.), conjuncts and other anaphoric adverbials (*so*, *therefore*, *accordingly*, *for this reason*, etc.), and various 'clause-integrated' expressions with a similar function (*that's why*, *the reason/result was*, etc.). The results that are of greatest interest here can be summarized as follows (cf. Table 6.1):

(a) Of the 63 lexical, grammatical and positional connective types recorded in the material, 57 occurred in the written corpus, but only 35 in the spoken corpus; at the same time there were almost twice as many tokens in the spoken as in the written material. In other words, the type/token ratio of causal connecters was much higher in the written corpus. To give some examples from the most common types: while the spoken material was found to rely heavily on two connecters, *because* and *so*, which accounted for no less than 80 per cent of all the connecters in the spoken data, the same types represented only 22 per cent in the written material; hence there was much greater stylistic variation in the written corpus (e.g. *because* 15 per cent, *for* 13 per cent, *therefore* 11 per cent, *since* 8 per cent, *thus* 8 per cent, *so* 7 per cent).

(b) On the whole, CR order and RC order were about equally common in the two corpora, but there was one notable exception: movable clauses of reason were much more rarely placed before their main clause in the spoken material.

Table 6.1 Distribution of causal connecters in a corpus of spoken (LLC) and written (LOB) English

Connecters	LLC	%	LOB	%	Total	%
because	366	49	66	15	432	37
so	233	31	30	7	263	22
other types	148	20	330	77	478	41
Total	747	100	426	100	1173	100

There is no doubt that these differences have their origin in the radically different communicative situations of the two text types. For example, it is obvious that the conditions of public writing (time for planning, the absence of an identifiable audience, etc.) foster a higher degree of style consciousness and channel orientation than those of spontaneous conversation, where factors like real-time planning, closer participant relation and a higher degree of message orientation combine to make stylistic variation superfluous or impossible (cf. Ochs 1979; Akinnaso 1982).

Lack of time for planning may also explain the greater avoidance of preposed adverbial clauses in the spoken corpus. Preposing a subordinate clause involves anticipation of the main clause, which seems to be a more difficult processing task than adding a subordinate clause 'retrospectively' (cf. the avoidance of nominal premodifiers in spoken discourse, as reported in Chafe 1982 and Kroch and Hindle 1982).

Other aspects of the results are more difficult to explain. For example, why should there be nearly twice as many causal expressions in spoken as in written discourse? Moreover, although CR and RC order were found to be about equally frequent in the two corpora (except in the case of mobile adverbial clauses), to what extent are these conditioned by the same contextual factors? On the whole, to what degree and in what ways do speech and writing favour different discourse strategies?

In the remainder of this article I will briefly examine these questions in the light of certain ordering principles that have been proposed in other studies, especially van Dijk 1977 and Winter 1982. I will concentrate on causal expressions linked by *because* and *so*, which are the most frequent pair of (potential) converses in the material as a whole, and therefore offer a promising basis of comparison. For reasons of space the emphasis will be on the spoken data, but the written material will remain in the background as an implicit contrast. I shall provide no statistics, since an analysis of discourse strategies does not lend itself easily to exact quantification. This does not mean that my observations are entirely impressionistic. They are based on a careful scrutiny of nearly 700 examples (cf. Table 6.1) in the fairly large and representative body of spoken and written material described above.

6.2 SOME PRINCIPLES OF LINEAR ORDERING

A suitable starting point for an analysis of causal sequencing strategies is van Dijk's (1977: 223 ff.) identification of four basic principles for presenting facts or events in a certain discourse order:

(a) NATURAL ORDERING: the sequence reflects the normal as real-world order of causal events, with the cause preceding its consequence;
(b) COGNITIVE ORDERING: the events or facts are presented in the order in which they catch the speaker's attention;
(c) THEMATIC ORDERING: events or facts presupposed to be known information are presented before those introducing new information;
(d) PRAGMATIC ORDERING: the presentation of events is determined by the speech act sequence (a *why*-question, for example, requires the listener to provide an explanation) or by the development of the discourse topic (the proposition that is closest to the current topic being presented first).

The operation of pragmatic ordering has been demonstrated in detail by Winter 1982, with special emphasis on the topical arrangement of adverbial clauses in written prose. Winter's summary of what he calls the 'contextual function' of the adverbial clause is worth quoting (p. 165):

Its main contextual function is to mediate between its main clause and the adjoining context of (independent) clause(s) in A CHANGE OF TOPIC WHICH IS MOST LIKELY TO BE

DEVELOPED FURTHER BY THE NEXT IMMEDIATE (INDEPENDENT) CLAUSE(S). In front-position, the adverbial clause picks up the topic of the preceding clause(s) while its main clause introduces the change of topic. Here the adverbial clause concludes the preceding topic. In end-position, the main clause now picks up and concludes the topic of the preceding clause(s) while its adverbial clause introduces the change of topic. Here the adverbial clause initiates the new topic.

Adverbial clauses in mid-position, Winter assumes, do not affect the topic development of their main clause, but rather have a function similar to interpolative independent clauses.

Relating van Dijk's four principles to causal sequence, we can observe that natural ordering always results in CR order, while the other three may give rise to either CR or RC order, depending on the situation. Since *so*-sequences always involve CR order, while *because*-clauses generally expound RC order, the former are more likely to be used in naturally ordered discourse than the latter.

It should be added that the four ordering principles are also likely to interact in various ways, and that in many cases it may be difficult or impossible to determine which of them is most important. It is also probable that many other constraints will affect the presentation of causal events in discourse, for example, grammatical weight or complexity and factors relating to the planning process. Only the last of these will be considered here.

6.3 PRAGMATIC ORDERING

A scrutiny of the material shows that, of the four basic ordering principles, the pragmatic is by far the most important, in the spoken as well as the written corpus. In other words, causal relations are generally ordered in such a way that their members are in accord with the topic development in the discourse. This is demonstrated in the following example (on the prosodic notation, see Appendix):

(2)   A   797 [? ə:] ‖you can 'get all ᴧSȮRTS of 'things THÉRE■ · 798 ‖bought the ȦERIAL THÉRE■ – 799 but I ‖went down a 'couple of weeks ᴧLȦTER■ 800 when it ‖still 'wasn't [frns ə:] 'SATISFȦCTORY■ · 801 and I ‖asked for [ə] · I · ‖said · I ‖PRȈCED■ – 802 [ði:] ‖CȦBLE■ 803 (· coughs) I ‖said I ᴧwanted some coᴧaxial CȦBLE «as»■ · 804 ‖YȮU know■ 805 ‖what [?] I've · been ᴧusing on the 'old TAꞂ 'thing■ – 806 cos ‖I was SUSᴧPȈCIOUS■ 807 I've ‖still got a 'hope that 'ᴧthat's what's 'WRȮNG■ 808 be‖cause ▷[ðə] ‖YȮU know■ 809 [i] it was ‖in when we ᴧgot this ᴧHȮUSE■ 810 that that [tə] ‖TELEᴧVȈSION 'cable■

       B   811 ☆‖YȨAH■☆

     > A   812 ☆and of☆ ‖course the 'outside ᴧSHȨATH■ 813 is ‖ {RȨALLY 'got} ᴧBȦRED a 'lot■

       B   814 ‖[m̀]■

     > A   815 ‖being a'gainst a WȦLL■ 816 ‖YȮU know■ 817 ‖fifteen ᴧtwenty ‖probably 'twenty YȨARS■ 818 for ‖all {Ȉ} KNȮW■ – –

B   819 ☆‖«[m̄]»■☆

>A   820 ☆[ə:m]☆ of ‖wear and ⌂TĚAR on it■   821 ‖round the brick ⌂WÁLLS and 'things■

B   822 ‖«[m̄]»■ –

>A   823 ‖AND [ə:m]■ – 824 [ʌ] I ‖WÁNTED a 'longer 'length ÀNYWAY■   825 and you ‖can't 'really JÓIN it■   826 because there's ‖two ⌂CÒRES in it■ –

B   827 ‖NÒ■

A   828 «so you» ‖can't ⌂DÒ it■ –   829 ‖and SÒ [ə:m]■ ·   830 I ‖PRÍCED it■ · 831 and the ‖woman in THÈRE 'said the ‖chap's ⌂WÍFE■ ·   832 she ‖SÁID she was■ ·   833 ‖priced it ☆at ⌂ten ▷p☆   (LLC 1.7)

In this example, which occurs in a discussion of recording equipment, speaker A explains why he had to buy a new television cable. The passage gives a good illustration of the density of causal expressions in the spoken material. Apart from sequences that are not overtly signalled by a causal connecter, there are three postposed clauses of reason introduced by *cos* or *because* (TU 806, 808, 826) and two result clauses introduced by *so* (TU 828, 829). These can all be explained as pragmatically ordered (the *so*-clauses also illustrate natural ordering), the sequence being determined by the topic development in the discourse. For example, the *cos*-clause in TU 806 must follow its antecedent in TU 803, which develops the topic of the cable introduced in preceding context. At the same time it connects naturally with the following context, which continues the new topic introduced by the *cos*-clause itself: why speaker A was suspicious. The same pragmatic constraints apply to the other causal sequences in the passage, although in some cases other principles are at work as well. I will return to these later.

As Winter has demonstrated, the topic dependency of causal (and other) sequences can be tested by a reversal of the clauses involved, replacing the sequence by its converse paraphrase ('R *because* C'—'C *so* R' and vice versa). In (2) this produces contextually impossible or awkward results, precisely because it destroys the topic development of the passage.

However, although pragmatic ordering predominates in both corpora, it is natural that speech and writing should favour different TYPES of pragmatic influence. While the written texts are generally planned with care, often with a manifest concern for rhetorical organization (involving topic sentences at the beginning or end of paragraphs, syntactic parallelism, etc.), the unfolding of the topic in spontaneous conversation tends to be 'globally' unplanned, capricious and meandering, yet 'locally' constrained by the speech act sequence or by the interaction of the participants. This latter feature is illustrated in the following examples, where the choice of causal expression is determined by the previous speaker's utterance:

(3)   **B**   443 ‖is it a ⌂REA⌂LÍSTIC 'book■

      A   444 ‖NÒ■ ·   445 ‖I' don't 'think so■

      B   446 ‖WHỲ not■ – –   447 ‖PÁCKED with DÉTAIL■ – – –

      A   448 because I ‖don't 'think it's a situ'ation «that would» – ARÍSE■

B   449 ‖why has he MÁDE it do 'then∎ –

A   450 because he ‖wants to SHǑW∎ · 451 what ‖people can 'do under 'certain ᴧCÌRCUMSTANCES∎   (LLC 3.1)

Another speech-specific feature illustrating this local pragmatic constraint is the high frequency of causal disjuncts (see Quirk *et al.* 1972: 752), which give the reason for a previous speech act (e.g. 'I ask this because . . .'):

(4)   B   39 ✰that's ‖INTERESTING∎✰ 40 ‖how ǑLD is 'he∎ · 41 cos ‖I ▷found this ▷very ▷difficult to ᴧGÙESS∎ 42 on ‖LǑOKING ✰at him∎✰   (LLC 1.6)

As Winter has pointed out (1982: 165), topically determined sequences are often tied both forwards and backwards in discourse. However, this is more typical of written texts, where the progression of discourse is premeditated and part of an organized whole. In spontaneous conversation, where planning is never far ahead of execution, pragmatically ordered sequences cannot be determined by the following context. Impromptu speakers are rarely capable of anticipating a topic (except in very general terms); rather, they seem to order their utterances retrospectively in accordance with the preceding context. (In turn-taking a speaker cannot of course predict the next speaker's contribution; the point here is that he seldom seems to anticipate his own utterances.) A revealing illustration of this phenomenon is the tendency in the spoken texts to arrange causal expressions in interlocking sequences, which are initiated by a preliminary reason, often couched in general terms, and subsequently specified by a more precise reason:

(5)   >A   33 ‖then [ə] ✰✰- and✰✰ ‖then he [əːh] · 'sent a

      B   36 ✰✰《3 to 4 sylls》✰✰

      >A   33 ᴧMÈSSAGE∎ · 37 《‖by》 'Stanley 'Johnson 'saying 《can I》 'come at FǑUR∎ 38 ✰《3 to 4 sylls》✰

      B   39 ✰《but this was✰ BE‖CÀUSE∎》 40 of ‖MÈ∎ 41 be‖cause ᴧI 'said I '《wanted》 to ᴧGÒ at 'four THÍRTY {I ✰‖THÍNK∎} ∎✰   (LLC 1.4)

(6)   in ᴧactual 'fact of 'course their ᴧcentral 'ᴧHÉATING 'oil∎ · 373 is '‖PRÓBABLY∎ 374 '‖RǑUGHLY∎ 375 a‖bout the ᴧsame 'price as ᴧÒURS∎ 376 because ‖we're 'not [əm] for ‖very CHÉAP 'oil∎ · 377 we ‖pay a▷bout ᴧtwenty–two 'pence a GÀLLON∎ 378 ‖DÒN'T we∎ 379 for ✰‖ÒURS∎✰

      C   380 ✰‖I THÍNK so∎✰ 381 I ‖can't +REMÉMBER NÓW∎+

      B   382 +‖YÈS∎+

      a   383 that all –

      B   384 '‖YÈS∎ 385 because it ‖doesn't 'bear TÁX on it∎

      a   386 《[m · m]》 ✰《1 to 2 sylls》✰

      B   387 ✰and✰ they ‖DÒ THÍS∎ 388 be‖cause such a ᴧlot of 'things 'like [əːm] – after ‖all ELECᴧTRÍCITY SÚB'STATIONS∎ 389 and ‖《goodness》 STÁTIONS∎ 390 and ‖goodness 'knows what ÈLSE 'burn ÓIL∎ 391 and ‖this 《would》 – 'make

ᴧÍNDUSTRY■ ³⁹² so ‖absolutely 'UN'ᴧPRÓFITABLE■ ³⁹³ ‖if you – ‖if you 'put a
ᴧTÁX on it■ ³⁹⁴ or ‖MÙCH ☆«of a tax■»☆   (LLC 1.13)

The procedure used by the speakers in these cases is to plunge into the first
explanation that comes into their minds, but realizing that this is not
sufficiently detailed, they add one or several more specific explanations. The
same extemporizing, 'stepwise' way of reasoning is also illustrated (2) above,
where speaker A ends up with two major reasons for buying the cable, but
where each reason is reached through a series of explanatory steps, each
specifying the previous one. The result is a succession of pragmatically ('non-
naturally'— ordered RC sequences, realized by postposed *because*-clauses or
by clauses without an overt causal connecter (the pattern is roughly: X *cos* A
(because) B *because* C *and* (so) D *being* F *and* Y *and* (= because) F *because* G *so*
F *and so* X). There is no doubt that this improvised discourse 'strategy'
contributes to the higher density of causal expressions in the spoken material.

6.4 NATURAL ORDERING

The influence of natural ordering is more difficult to demonstrate. It always
results in CR sequences, realized as *so*-clauses or, exceptionally, preposed
because-clauses. Since it normally cooperates with pragmatic ordering, it can
only be revealed as an independent strategy in cases where no alternative
explanation is at hand, or where it clearly overrules other strategies.

Natural ordering ought to be especially appropriate in narrative contexts
(with temporal sequencing) or in contexts characterized by deductive
reasoning (logical sequencing). Discourse types of this kind cut across the
spoken–written contrast, and there is nothing in the material to suggest that
they should be more prevalent in either medium. Yet here I want to call
attention to another speechspecific phenomenon related to the improvised
discourse procedure discussed in the previous section. In impromptu speech,
a speaker is not always immediately aware of the causal relationship of the
events or facts he is about to describe. A recurrent strategy in such cases is
therefore that the speaker starts with an account of the premises of a causal
situation, often in narrative terms, and then draws the relevant conclusions
retrospectively (or deductively).

In (7) below, a former medical student gives an account of his achievement
in a clinical examination. His main point is that he did well because he
happened to have read about the kind of case he was asked to comment on.
But instead of saying so straight away ('I did well because . . .'), which would
have been pragmatically appropriate, he reverses the sequence, presenting the
background before the consequence. This 'narrative' strategy (demonstrated
repeatedly by the same speaker elsewhere in the text) is in fact used twice in
the quoted passage, and results in a naturally ordered chain containing three
so-clauses (and two coordinated clauses linked by *and* (TU 13), which is here
equivalent to resultative 'so'):

(7)   A   ¹ I ‖had a ∆very very ∆RÁRE condition∎ - ² [ə:m?] it was [ə:] I ‖had a
∆PAEDIÀTRIC · a ‖KÍDDY∎ · ³ a ‖KÍDDY 'thing∎ ⁴ ‖YǑU know∎ · ⁵ and it
‖was [ə:m] - «and» there are ‖only about [?] ∆TWÈNTY of ▷these∎ ⁶ a ‖YÈAR∎
· ⁷ ocⅠcur a YÈAR∎ ⁸ «(of the)» par‖ticular ∆PRÒBLEM I 'had∎ · ⁹ and ‖I
happen«ed» to have ˙∆RÉAD a'bout it∎ ¹⁰ aⅠbout a ∆YÈAR a'go∎ · ¹¹ so I
‖knew 'quite a 'lot A˙∆BÒUT it you ▷see∎ · ¹² it's ‖not the sort of ▷thing - ·
I'd ‖seen 'one 'patient on a ∆WÀRD with it∎ ¹³ and I thought ‖ÒH∎ · ¹⁴ I'll
‖RÉAD a'bout {‖THÀT∎}∎ - ¹⁵ ‖so I ∆RÉAD a'bout it∎ ¹⁶ so I ‖knew quite a
'lot A∆BÒUT it you SÉE∎   (LLC 2.9)

The following two examples illustrate the same extemporizing procedure;
in both a conclusion is reached via an introductory preamble:

(8)   C   ²⁹⁰ ☆‖is☆ the FÍRM 'paying 'for him∎ -
      B   ²⁹¹ well he's ‖only he was ‖only a ∆LǑGGER∎ - ²⁹² [di] he was ‖only a '[kʌ] a
∆FÒREST worker∎ ²⁹³ ‖so +I ∆shouldn't «THÍNK it was∎»+   (LLC 1.13)

(9)   B   the ∆PRÒVOST is ad'dressing us TOMÓRROW∎
      B   ¹¹⁰¹ «‖ÍSN'T he∎» ¹¹⁰² have you ‖sÉEN that∎
      A   ¹¹⁰³ ‖NÒ∎
      B   ¹¹⁰⁴ ‖at the 'faculty of ∆ÀRTS∎ ¹¹⁰⁵ ‖it's a ∆special ∆MÉETING 'he's
ADDRÉSSING∎ ¹¹⁰⁶ up‖on the ▷allo▷cation of RE∆SÒURCES∎ ¹¹⁰⁷ «it» ‖SÁYS∎
¹¹⁰⁸ we ‖had a 'notice in the ∆middle of the «∆THÍNG∎»
      A   ¹¹⁰⁹ ‖where was the ∆NÒTICE∎ -
      B   ¹¹¹⁰ ‖well it 'came 'round in the ∆VÀC SÒME 'time∎ - -
      A   ¹¹¹¹ ‖I ☆∆must «GÒ»∎☆
      B   ¹¹¹² ☆«yeah» at the '‖last☆ 'faculty of ÀRTS ▷meeting∎ ¹¹¹³ they ‖said they'd
∆ÀSK the ▷provost∎ ¹¹¹⁴ to ‖come to the ∆next MÈETING∎ ¹¹¹⁵ but ‖he
˙∆can't CÒME∎ ¹¹¹⁶ ‖so they've 'got this ˙∆ÈXTRA 'meeting ÒN∎ ¹¹¹⁷ ‖just for
∆THÌS∎   (LLC 1.4)

The influence of natural ordering is particularly clear in passages which
reveal a change in the planning process. In the following examples the speaker
launches into an utterance but realizes in mid-execution that an explanation
is called for, and so ends up with a naturally ordered CR sequence:

(10)   B   they ‖came ∆BÀCK 'after a MÓNTH∎ ⁷⁵⁰ they ‖said well it's all
∆{RÌGHT} for a - a winter HÓLIDAY∎ - ⁷⁵¹ cos ‖they're very ∆ÀCTIVE
'people∎ ⁷⁵² and ‖they [n] - · [?ə] ‖I ∆think 'her FÁMILY∎ ⁷⁵³ were ‖vaguely
∆farmers and ∆LÀNDOWNERS∎ ⁷⁵⁴ ‖round ABÒUT∎   (LLC 1.13)

(11)   A   ²¹³ and he ‖said well ∆how old do you 'think this
∆CHÌLD is you SÉE∎ - - - ²¹⁴ and I ‖didn't 'have a ∆CLÙE∎ · ²¹⁵ ‖you SÉE∎

216 ‖it was a [?] ‖it was a [?] · it was it was an ‖ÀSIAN 'child■ 217 be‖tween
the ∆age of · ‖it was ∆STÁNDING 'up■ 218 so ‖therefore it was 'thirteen
MÒNTHS■ · 219 to ‖FÓUR YÈARS■ 220 I ‖didn't ∆really – «you» ‖see the
∆thing WÀS■ · 221 that ‖ {RÈNAL 'rickets} OC∆CÙRS■ 222 at the ‖age of – the
‖age of a'bout ∆THRÈE you 'see■ · 223 ‖SÒ■ · 224 the ‖kid is al ▷ready
∆STÀNDING■ – 225 so ‖THÈREFORE■ 226 they ‖get ∆very ▷very BÓWED LÈGS■
(LLC 2.9)

(12) a   1001 ☆and that it's up☆ to you to keep on reading and working all the time
show that you can be a full-time student before you become a full-time
☆ ☆student☆ ☆

A   1002 ☆ ☆‖YÈS■☆ ☆ ·

a   1003 OK ·

A   1004 ‖well I'm ∆giving ∆NÒTICE■ – 1005 «to ‖finish» my 'job in ∆ÁPRIL■
1006 so ‖I shall be – be‖cause my FI∆NÀNCES■ 1007 will ‖work 'out from a∆bout
that TÍME■ 1008 ‖so I shall 'have – – ∆April and ˙MÁY■ (LLC 3.1)

Natural ordering rarely affects *because*-clauses, which are mainly preposed
on thematic grounds (section 6.5). However, in the following example it seems
that natural ordering has prevailed—the preposed *because*-clause cannot be
explained on either thematic or pragmatic grounds (the consequence being in
fact both thematically and pragmatically closer to the preceding context):

(13) B   610 ‖I did 'know ∆one ▷Indian 'who · ∆I∆RÒNICALLY■ – 611 ‖learnt to
CHÁIN'SMOKE■ 612 ‖in this ∆CÒUNTRY■ 613 it ‖seemed ABSÙRD■

A   614 (– ☆–☆ laughs)

B   615 ☆he ‖CÁME☆ HÉRE■ 616 ‖when he was ∆just 'after ∆FÓRTY■ – 617 ‖and ·
∆did a couple of 'years RESÈARCH■ 618 at ‖CÁMBRIDGE■ 619 «in»
‖MATHEMÁTICS■ – – 620 and ‖basically be∆cause he was ∆LÒNELY■ – ·
621 ‖he ▷started [tʃ] · smoking ‖ {NÒT I sup'pose} ∆CHÁIN'SMOKING 'but■ ·
622 ‖PRÈTTY ∆HÉAVILY■ (LLC 1.6)

6.5 THEMATIC ORDERING

The principle of thematic ordering is well described in grammars. Its effect on
causal relations tends to coincide with both pragmatic and natural ordering,
since the contextually given element is often retrievable from the preceding
topic and presented as a logical premise. Yet clear instances of thematic
ordering are comparatively rare in the material.

Thematic ordering may give rise to both CR and RC sequences. Here I will
concentrate on a few examples illustrating its effect on *because*-clauses. In (14)
two teachers are discussing the value of précis testing and what may happen to
students who 'lift' too much of the original text:

(14) > B   ☆ ☆ – ☆ ☆   968 ‖if they lift too
          MÚCH of

      A   969 ☆‖YÉS■☆   970 ☆ ☆‖YÉS■   971 ‖QUÍTE■☆ ☆

      > B   968 ▷it■   972 ‖they penalise THEM△SÉLVES■ ☆ · ☆

      A   973 ☆‖YÉS■☆

      > B   974 be‖cause they run out of △WÒRDS■

      A   975 be‖cause △then it it sends them △chasing AWÁY■ ·   976 to ‖find △quite ·
          MERE△TRÍCIOUS · [əːm] {‖SÙBSTITUTES for ▷words■} ■

      B   977 ‖ABSO△LÙTELY■   978 and in ‖IMÀNY cases of CÓURSE■   979 the ‖words ☆can
          '△NÒT {be ‖SÙBSTITUTE■} ■☆

      A   980 ☆《2 sylls · 1 syll · 》‖no QUÍTE■☆ ·   981 ‖YÉS■

      B   982 and ‖very ÓFTEN■   983 you ‖get a △student 'who · △probably △DÓES
          understand the PÁSSAGE■ ·   984 but be‖cause he feels he △MÙSTN'T use the
          ☆words of☆ the PÁSSAGE■ ☆ ☆–☆ ☆   985 ‖gives

      A   986 ☆《‖QUÍTE■》☆   987 ☆ ☆《‖YÉS■》☆ ☆

      > B   985 you the im△pression that he ☆△DÔESN'T under△stand it■☆ –   988 be‖cause
          he's △used words which △aren't so △GÔOD■   (LLC 1.1)

The *because*-clauses in TU 984 and TU 988 straddle the same main clause
(TU 985), which is coordinated with the clause in TU 983. The main clauses
present new information (with contrastive focus), while the *because*-clauses
contain information that is contextually given or taken for granted. The
example is interesting because it gives some indication of what factors may
determine the choice between different ordering principles. Why has
thematic ordering affected the first clause rather than the second (or both)? A
possible answer is the degree of 'givenness' of the two clauses and the
combination of forethought and improvisation that seems to characterize the
passage. Of the two *because*-clauses the first is obviously taken more for
granted (it expresses the prerequisite for the entire discussion), while the
second repeats the rather distant content of TU 975 and conveys sufficient
additional information to be eligible for final position. Moreover, a preposed
subordinate clause anticipates its main clause and consequently requires
some foresight. The main clause in TU 985 is obviously to some extent
premeditated, being contrastively anticipated by TU 983, while the final
because-clause seems to be the least preplanned unit and added pragmatically
almost as an afterthought.

Thematic fronting serves to bring new information into end-focus (cf.
Quirk *et al.* 1972: 945 ff.). A more marked effect can be achieved by clefting,
which highlights an emphatic or contrastive element as complement in a
copular clause while leaving the thematically given element in the 'shade'. A
rare instance of this construction is the following example:

(15) B   105 ☆《oh I ‖haven't △heard ÁNYTHING■》☆   106 well ‖Mallet is is [ə] is
          △hopping MÁD■   107 a‖bout all THÍS■   108 because ‖Mallet sees a △hundred
          and fifty thousand pounds for a △BÚILDING■   109 and ‖various △other things

ᴬgoing down the DRÁIN∎ –   ¹¹⁰ ‖what ∆I [f] «what» ‖î'think∎   ¹¹¹ he ‖doesn't
ᴬRÉALIZE∎   ¹¹² is that · it's ‖very largely BECÁUSE {he's ‖been BÙILDING∎ ·
[ə:m?] ‖this kind of PERÍPHERAL ▷thing∎} ∎   ¹¹³ ‖in «ÁPPLEBY∎»   ¹¹⁴ that it
‖HÀS «gone down∎»   (LLC 1.2)

Here both the *because*-clause and the postposed *that*-clause convey given
information. What is in focus is the causal relation as such, a fact which is
marked by prosodic emphasis on the connecter.

However, it is easy to find examples in which pragmatic ordering prevails
over thematic ordering. This is especially the case when the given element is
contextually distant:

(16)   C   ¹¹⁹⁹ ☆[ə:m]☆ there's ‖so much [?]ᴬÉLSE to 'do in 'London∎   ¹²⁰⁰ +you ‖don't+
           ∆WÀNT to 'hang a'bout∎ ·   ¹²⁰¹ ‖this PLÁCE∎

     A   ¹²⁰² +‖I KNÒW∎+

  >C   ¹²⁰³ be‖cause ∆as we SÁID∎   ¹²⁰⁴ it's ‖not very 'nice to ᴬSTÀY in∎ · (LLC 3.3)

By contrast, situationally given elements (referring to physically present
objects) have a strong ordering effect, as in the following example where two
speakers are comparing pictures displayed in front of them:

(17)   C   ⁴⁸⁶ ☆‖NÒ∎☆ ·   ⁴⁸⁷ and ‖this is too BÍG∎   ⁴⁸⁸ or just ‖not +[ə:]+

     A   ⁴⁸⁹ +[ə:]+ ‖THÀT one∎   ⁴⁹⁰ I ‖definitely 'thought I'm ᴬnot 'going to ᴬHÀVE∎
           ⁴⁹¹ be‖cause I would 'find the ᴬcolours DEPRÈSSING∎   (LLC 1.8)

6.6 COGNITIVE ORDERING

In (17) thematic and cognitive ordering seem to merge: what is situationally
given is also cognitively prominent. Cognitive ordering is on the whole
extremely difficult to establish as an independent factor in the material, since
there is generally no way of knowing what is uppermost in the speaker's mind
at a given moment. Possible exceptions are the abrupt changes of topic that
now and then take place in spontaneous conversation:

(18)   C   ²⁶⁵ by the ‖WÀY 'Barry∎   ²⁶⁶ they've ‖got that 'piece a'bout 'Larchmold ᴬpinned
           ÙP∎   ²⁶⁷ in the ‖LEXIᴬCÒGRAPHY 'unit∎   ²⁶⁸ ☆so it ‖wasn't just ÙS∎☆ (LLC 2.14)

(19)   A   ²³¹ the the ‖best [ə:] ‖certainly what ᴬBritain ᴬdid in the ᴬSÈCOND World
           ▷War was [ə:]∎   ²³² I mean ‖I don't 'KNÒW∎   ²³³ I ‖merely REᴬPÈAT∎
           ²³⁴ what I've ‖read in ᴬBÒOKS∎   ²³⁵ ☆so I ‖don't really KNÒW∎   (LLC 2.3)

In these, the sudden introduction of a new (sub-) topic seems to be cognitively
determined, although, as the parenthetic interpolation in (19) demonstrates,
cognitive attention may also be triggered by some topical link.

6.7 REINFORCEMENT AND COOPERATIVE REDUNDANCY

A speech-specific trait that has been emphasized repeatedly in the preceding sections is the unpremeditated, rambling progression of conversational discourse. Despite the existence of 'local' ordering constraints, what is perhaps most striking in the spoken material is the 'global' lack of planning and foresight, and the way this affects the expression of causal relations. One such effect, already touched upon in section 6.4, is what I would like to call 'retrospective reinforcement'. A good example is (19) above, in which the speaker makes a comment (TU 232) which is not necessarily intended as a causal 'consequence' at the moment of speech, then adds an explanation, with or without an overt causal connecter (TU 233), and finally clinches the sequence by repeating the original utterance, now introduced by *so* (TU 235) to emphasize the conclusion to be drawn from the preceding utterances. In other words, the causal relationship of the first sequence is reinforced by a reversal around the second members, producing an interlocked RCR sequence. This strategy is very common in the spoken material:

(20) A   545 [ə:m · ə:] ‖even ▷at the ΔSCHŎOL ▷level∎ 546 where ‖pressure 'groups are
          'still ΔSTRŎNG∎ 547 because ‖parents Δstill want their Δbloody 'kids to 'go to
          · to ΔSCHŎOL∎

      B   548 ☆《‖YĔAH∎》☆

    > A   549 ☆if☆ ‖only 'to alΔlow · Δmum to go Δout to ˙ΔWŎRK∎ · 550 ‖YŎU
          know∎ – 551 [ə:m – ?] so the ‖pressure groups 'there are [st] are 'still STRŎNG∎
          (LLC 3.2)

(21) A   172 ☆I ‖must SĂY∎ 173 ‖I rang 'up☆ on ΔTHŬRSDAY∎ 174 be‖cause I Δhad a –
          LĔTTER∎ 175 an OF‖FĬCIAL 'letter∎ 176 ‖ĂGES a'go∎ 177 ‖from ☆☆[ə:] –☆☆
          ΔMiss ˙ΔBĂKER∎

      C   178 ☆☆《4 to 5 sylls》☆☆

    > A   179 ‖saying 'come at Δten O'ΔCLŎCK∎ 180 so I ‖RĂNG 《up saying》 I'm 'terribly
          SŎRRY∎ 181 but I ‖shan't be Δwith you until Δfive past ΔTĔN∎   (LLC 1.5)

As (21) indicates, *so*-clauses of this type may also serve to pick up the thread of discourse initiated by the first utterance (cf. Coulthard *et al.* 1981: 36). This subsidiary function, which becomes of primary importance when the intervening explanation develops into a long 'aside', is clearly demonstrated in (2), where two successive *so*-clauses occur in TU 828 and 829. While the first merely reinforces the proposition in TU 825, the second resumes the thread of discourse broken much earlier (in TU 801) by the long explanatory sequence discussed in section 6.3.

Retrospective reinforcement generally exhibits the pattern R + (*because*) C + *so* R, but occasionally the opposite pattern *because* (*of*) C + *so* R + *because* C occurs, where the final *because*-clause reinforces the first:

(22) A   343 yet ‖I [st] as ‖far as ˙ΔÍ know▪ 344 it's ‖just a parΔticular 'type of STÓUT▪
             345 which the ‖ÍRISH developed▪ 346 be‖cause of that 'marvellous WÀTER
             they've 'got▪ · 347 ‖so you ΔRÉALLY they · the ‖ÍRISHMEN 'say▪ 348 there's
             ‖no such ΔTHÌNG as the TRÚE thing in 'England▪ 349 be‖cause it's the
             ΔWÀTER▪ · (LLC 1.7)

Logically speaking, retrospective reinforcements tend to be redundant, since
they generally repeat contextually given information. In the examples given so
far only one of the causal members has been repeated, but the material also
contains many cases in which both members are contextually given. In such
instances, what is retrospectively emphasized is the causal relationship
between the given propositions (cf. example (15) above). Constructions of this
kind normally take the form of pragmatically determined *so*-clauses which
serve to sum up the preceding argument. Their reinforcing and summarizing
function is usually marked by an anaphoric causal expression (e.g. *that's why/
the reason for*) and by some lexical clarification. A few typical examples are:

(23) cos that's why he was CONDÙCTING (LLC 1.11.325)
      so this is why I'm floating RÒUND (LLC 1.5.1080)
      so that's why I'm about five minutes LĂTE you see (LLC 1.7.26)
      so [:] that's the reason for doing THÀT (LLC 3.2.996)
      so that's the PÌCTURE (LLC 2.6.1092)

The ultimate degree of redundancy is reached when *so* approaches the status
of a mere 'filler', suggesting that the speaker has little more to add:

(24) B   he ‖took 'Sam and 'I Δback to his · to ‖where he was ΔLÍVING▪ – 90 and ‖this
             was a FLÁT▪ 91 now ‖where WÀS it▪ – – · 92 ‖trouble 'is I Δdon't Δ{KNÒW
             north ▷London} at ΔÀLL▪
      A   93 ‖[m̀]▪
      B   94 and he ‖drove us 'there in a ΔCÀR▪ 95 ⋆so (– giggles)⋆ (LLC 1.6)

Yet, as I hope the examples have shown, it is misleading to call these
retrospective repetitions 'redundant'. Repetitions are a characteristic feature
of unplanned discourse (cf. Ochs 1979) and they generally have some
purposeful contextual function. Retrospective 'recyclings' of the kind
discussed here seem to have two major functions. One, which is speaker-
oriented, reflects the speaker's need to monitor his own speech and to keep
track of his own line of thought. The other, which is listener-oriented, reflects
the cooperative attitude that is an essential condition for successful communication: the speaker's positive attempt to clarify himself to his
interlocutors and to contribute to a smooth progression of discourse. Yet
whatever function they may have, there is no doubt that these recurrent
reinforcements are another important reason why causal expressions are
nearly twice as frequent in spontaneous conversation as in public writing.

6.8 CONCLUSION

In this chapter I have briefly examined the effect of four ordering principles on the use of two potentially converse causal expressions in spontaneous conversation. Obviously, nothing very conclusive can be derived from a limited and sketchy study of this kind, but certain tendencies in the material are either sufficiently clear or suggestive to be worth emphasizing.

Although the relative importance of the four ordering principles— PRAGMATIC, NATURAL, THEMATIC and COGNITIVE (with the pragmatic as the most powerful constraint)—appear to be roughly the same in the spoken and the written data, the interactive and unplanned character of spontaneous conversation favours certain speech-specific discourse strategies. Some of these are of 'local' character: pragmatic sequences determined by the interaction or, in the case of disjunct clauses, by a desire to justify a speech act. Others are more 'global' in the sense that they affect a succession of utterances in the same speaker's turn. To these belong:

(a) the stepwise reasoning resulting in pragmatically ordered sequences of successively more specific (postposed) *because*-clauses;
(b) pragmatically and naturally ordered 'narrative' *so*-sequences, initiated by an introductory preamble;
(c) 'retrospective reinforcement', also determined by a combination of pragmatic and natural ordering, resulting in a final *so*-clause which serves to clarify or sum up a preceding argument or to pick up the thread of discourse after an explanatory aside.

These 'global' speaker strategies have some features in common with the way a writer organizes his paragraphs, but in contrast to the carefully planned units of public writing, the spoken 'paragraphs' derive their character from the unpremeditated, rambling and largely retrospective progression of impromptu speech. It is against this background that the frequent use of causal expressions in spontaneous conversation can best be understood. Despite the many implicit connections characteristic of spoken discourse, the constant extemporizing also forces the impromptu speaker to signal, overtly and repeatedly, the various links and twists in his chain of thought, for the benefit of himself as well as of his audience.

The causal connecters *because* and *so* play important roles in this process. The first, the more common of the two, nearly always initiates a postposed clause of reason, which expands the content of a pragmatically (topically) tied main clause. *So*-clauses, although somewhat less frequent, serve a greater variety of functions in pragmatically and naturally ordered sequences— conveying consequences of previous events, deductively drawn conclusions, summarizing previous arguments, or picking up a broken thread of discourse.

APPENDIX

Symbols used in the transcription of the spoken material (from Svartvik and Quirk 1980: 21 f.).

TEXT NUMBER	S.2.3 S.3.1a	Text number; small letter denotes subtext (example)	NUCLEUS	yĔs	Fall
				yɛ́s	Rise
SPEAKER	A	Speaker identity (example)		yɛ̄s	Level
	>A	Speaker identity; speaker continues where he left off (example)		yɛ̆s	(Rise-) fall-rise
				yɛ̂s	(Fall-) rise-fall
	A, B	A and B (example)		yĔs yɛ́s	Fall-plus-rise
	A/B	A or B (example)		yɛ́s yĔs	Rise-plus-fall
	VAR	Various speakers	BOOSTER	▷ yes	Continuance
	?	Speaker identity unknown		△ yes	Higher than preceding syllable
	a	Non-surreptitious speaker (example)		△ yes	Higher than preceding pitch-prominent syllable
	☆ yes ☆ +yes+	Simultaneous talk		△ yes	Very high
	(laughs)	Contextual comment	STRESS	'yes	Normal
	«yes»	Incomprehensible words		'yes	Heavy
TONE UNIT	■	End of tone unit (TU)	PAUSE	yes · yes	Brief pause (of one light syllable)
	‖	Onset		yes — yes	Unit pause (of one stress unit or 'foot')
	{yes}	Subordinate TU		_ ·	
				_ _	Combinations of pause
				_ _ ·	
				_ _ _	

7 What does *really* really do?

Anna-Brita Stenström
Lund University, Sweden

7.1 INTRODUCTION

Really belongs to a category of discourse words whose meaning and function vary from syntactically significant to interactively expressive. Some uses of *really* are common to speech and writing; these uses are defined and described in grammars. Other uses are characteristic of speech alone and have only been partly described. Although I am fully aware of the difficulties involved, and by no means claim to solve all the problems, I will try to give a brief survey of what I think *really* does in written and spoken discourse, with special emphasis on spoken discourse, since it is the least investigated area.

Five basic functions may be identified. These may roughly be looked upon as constituting points on two parallel and partly overlapping scales, one representing the syntactic level, the other the interactional level, and with the third line representing the planning process, connecting the two (see Figure 7.1).

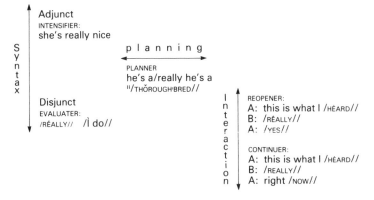

Figure 7.1 Discourse functions

As an intensifier, integrated in the clause structure and placed next to a head, *really* fills an adverbial slot and is part of a syntactic unit. As an evaluator it is peripheral to the clause structure and reflects the writer/speaker's attitude to the entire predication (cf. the distinction between adjunct and disjunct in Quirk *et al.* 1972). At the interactional level, *really* is a conversational device which may or may not affect the turn-taking system; as a reopener it expresses the speaker's reaction to what was said by the previous speaker and elicits a response, thereby causing speaker-shift; as a continuer (for this term see Schegloff 1982) *really* shows the hearer's active participation and signals to the current speaker to go on talking. At the level of planning, finally, it is a speech-specific device which is partly possible to describe in syntactic terms.

Traditionally, *really* has been regarded as an adverb which either intensifies an element of clause or reflects the speaker/writer's attitude to an entire proposition. But the traditional description of *really* does not cover all its functions, notably in conversation. What makes *really* so difficult to define is the fact that it behaves differently from any other item classified as an adverb. Not only is it more mobile within the sentence; it can fill any of the following slots:

—it—is—not—as bad—as you—think—

It also occurs as a separate prosodic unit, in which capacity it is closely associated with the turn-taking system.

To begin with I shall show how *really* occurs in relation to other elements in a syntactic environment and then try to provide some suggestions about what it appears to do from a strategic and interactive point of view.

7.2 DATA

The *Lancaster–Oslo/Bergen Corpus of Spoken English* (LOB) (see Hofland and Johansson 1982) served as a data basis for the written material and the *London–Lund Corpus of Spoken English* (LLC) (see Svartvik *et al.* 1982) for the spoken material.

Since I already knew, from checking the LOB and LLC concordances, that *really* occurred much more frequently in speech than in writing, I restricted myself to a reduced version of the LLC corpus, consisting of approximately 170,00 words, but used the entire LOB corpus of approximately one million words. The reduced corpus is composed of 34 surreptitiously recorded, spontaneous, face-to-face conversations, with the number of speakers varying from two to six. The speakers are British: academic staff, department secretaries and students. The topics range from curriculum planning to contraceptives. The LOB corpus includes different genres of prose: newspaper text, miscellaneous informative prose, learned and scientific articles and fiction.

I did not aim at a maximal contrast between spoken and written production; in that case I would have excluded fiction, which is bound to contain features of speech in the dialogues. But since it might be assumed that *really* would have a different distribution in informative prose than in fiction, I also wanted to check that aspect.

Really occurred with a density of 0.31 per 1,000 words in LOB and 3.17 per 1,000 words in LLC (where it occupies rank 59; see Svartvik *et al.* 1982—a considerable difference which immediately indicates that *really* is a characteristic feature of conversation. It might be mentioned in this connection that the remaining 53 conversations in the larger LLC corpus, in which discussions and public and prepared speeches dominate, contained 1.90 instances of *really* per 1,000 words. In LOB, the density was higher in the fiction category (0.55) than in the informative category (0.23 per 1,000 words).

In order to make a fair comparison between LLC and LOB possible, I picked a random sample consisting of 100 instances of *really* from each corpus, a procedure which was facilitated by the availability of the concordance versions of the corpora.

7.3 POSITION IN CLAUSE

If prosodic features are disregarded, the majority of the 200 instances of *really* can be fairly adequately described in syntactic terms on the basis of their position in the utterance. Some uses are ambiguous, however, and others are better described in pragmatic and/or interactive terms.

For the syntactic description I looked at the way *really* occurred in declarative, interrogative and what I will call 'speech-specific' utterances. The distribution in the data was as shown in Table 7.1. It may seem odd that there were more interrogatives in writing than in speech. Three factors should be kept in mind in this regard: one is that most interrogatives in LOB were rhetorical questions; a second that the written data included fiction where questions occurred in the dialogues; and a third that *really* alone, functioning as a question, is hidden in the 'speech-specific' category (see Section 7.6).

Table 7.1 *Really* in three types of utterance

	W	S	Total
Declarative	89	84	173
Interrogative	11	5	16
Speech-specific	—	11	11
Total	100	100	200

It was immediately obvious that *really* collocates with negation (NEG), generally realized by *not* but sometimes by other non-assertive items, such as *nobody*, *without* and *only*. Therefore I made a first distinction between *really* in positive and negative utterances (Table 7.2). In the five missing cases *really* constituted the entire utterance. Negative utterances were more common in the spoken sample, positive in the written sample. This was expected and is in accordance with the findings of Tottie and Paradis 1982 who investigated spoken and written data in the *Survey of English Usage* material. Moreover, it

Table 7.2 *Really* in positive and negative utterances

	W	S	Total
Declarative			
Positive	66	56	122
Negative	23	28	51
Interrogative			
Positive	10	5	15
Negative	1	—	1
Speech-specific			
Positive	—	4	4
Negative	—	2	2
Total	100	95	195

appeared that *really* was slightly more frequent with NEG in speech than in writing.

The dominating position of *really* in negative declaratives is illustrated below (for the term operator (op) see Quirk *et al.* 1972: 65):

| S op n't REALLY pred |

W: 22
S: 26

I haven't *really* concentrated

I don't *really* relish the thought

It isn't *really* all

The number of occurrences of *really* after NEG compared to the few instances in other places is revealing. There were only two other types (three tokens), one with *really* placed between subject and operator and the other with *really* placed in final position. Quirk *et al.* (1972: 442) deal with *really* in negative clauses in terms of scope. *Really* is either within the scope of negation, as in 'I don't *really* know him', which is paraphrased by 'It's not the real truth that I know him', or lies without, as in 'I *really* don't know him', rewritten 'The real truth is that I don't know him'. The fact that *really* in post-NEG position was preferred in both the written and the spoken data seems to indicate that both writers and speakers prefer denying the truth of a proposition to asserting that the proposition is false, a strategy which makes it possible to avoid being too straightforward. More or less emphasis may be employed in speech. Compare, for example:

(1) I /can't really 'go and :do all 'that the 'next :mĭnute//   1.10:596
(2) ((it's just)) that I /don't "rĕally 'relish the 'thought//
    of /going through :spàin// (((/hònestly//))   2.13:611

In (1), where *really* is unmarked for prosody, I suggest that it acts as a softener and is equivalent to 'you know' and in (2) that it serves to contradict what he judges to be the hearer's assumption, roughly corresponding to 'to tell you the truth'.

The configurations of *really* in positive declaratives were much more complex and varied. But the dominating position was immediately after the operator, that is, the same as in negative declaratives, but for NEG:

S op REALLY pred	W: 33

S: 22

I have *really* got a bug about it

They were *really* devastating

The most interesting variant was:

S op pred REALLY	W: 1

S: 16

Ileen has forgotten that *really*

It's all mad *really*

which indicates that *really* in clause-final position is much more common in speech than in writing (see Section 7.5). This tendency was confirmed in the larger corpora. But it is worth pointing out that *really* very seldom occurred in final position in negative utterances, where it generally preferred post-NEG position.

As to interrogatives, the position of *really* in the two media is not directly comparable due to the different realizations of the interrogative form. Interrogatives in writing had inverted word order, whereas interrogatives in speech were in the form of tag-Qs:

$$\left\{ \begin{matrix} \text{DO(n't)} \\ \text{BE} \end{matrix} \right\} \text{ S REALLY Pred} \qquad \begin{matrix} \text{W: 11} \\ \text{S: 5} \end{matrix}$$

Don't you *really* know?

Are you *really* happy with him?

$$\left\{ \begin{matrix} \text{V} \\ \text{BE} \end{matrix} \right\} \text{ REALLY } \left\{ \begin{matrix} \text{A} \\ \text{C} \end{matrix} \right\} \text{ tag} \qquad \begin{matrix} \text{W: 0} \\ \text{S: 4} \end{matrix}$$

goes on *really* regularly doesn't it

it was *really* convincing wasn't it

Since the number of interrogatives in the two samples was too small to suggest with any certainty which interrogative form dominated in each medium and where *really* was generally positioned, I examined all the instances of *really* in interrogatives in LOB and the reduced version of LLC and found that the tendencies manifested in the samples were confirmed.

7.4 POSITION AND SYNTACTIC FUNCTION

What does *really* do in the various positions? And to what extent can position be taken as a criterion of syntactic function?

Bolinger 1972 describes how *really*, among a number of other sentence adverbs, had undergone a gradual change from truth identifier to intensifier. He regards the intensifying function as a result of a grammatical shift involving a reassortment of sentence constituents so that what was originally an emphasis on the whole 'dictum' is converted into an emphasis on some part of it (cf. 1972: 94–5). His example is *truly*, which he says is more readily taken as a premodifier of an adjective the closer it gets to the normal position of a premodification. As to *really*, it has developed into a 'pure' intensifier, reflected in the form *real*, as in 'she's real nice', which shows no trace of the identifying function.

The fact that the form *real* was not found with intensifying function in these data can most certainly NOT be taken as an indication that *really* in this very form can never serve as a pure intensifier in British English.

Quirk *et al.* (1972: 440) remark in this connection that 'emphasizers' (their term for the subcategory of intensifiers which includes *really*) that are placed next to a particular element and are not separated by intonation or punctuation often emphasize that part alone, but that there is ambivalence as to whether the emphasis is on the part or on the whole.

The problem is highlighted in the following examples:

(3) (a) this Q is *really* surprising
    (b) this is a *really* surprising Q
    (c) this is *really* a surprising Q
    (d) this *really* is a surprising Q
    (e) *really* this is a surprising Q
    (f) this is a surprising Q *really*

Disregarding the possible effect of prosody and punctuation, it may safely be stated that when *really* is placed next to the adjective, it is clearly an intensifier which serves to modify 'surprising'. But the further it is moved towards the left, the less emphasis is on the part, 'surprising', and the more is on the whole, 'a surprising Q'. In (2e), where *really* is placed in utterance-initial position, it no longer intensifies a single clause element or unit but comments on the entire proposition.

Greenbaum 1969, who defines *really* in terms of 'intensifier' and 'disjunct', states that *really* is unambiguously a disjunct in initial position and also usually when it occurs in a separate tone unit. As a disjunct it 'makes explicit the speaker's view that the statement being made is true' (1969: 144). Quirk *et al.* 1972 provide a similar description but add that what they call 'attitudinal' disjuncts may also express the speaker's attitude to the previous speaker's utterance.

Initial position was infrequent indeed, only one instance in each sample. This tendency was confirmed in the larger corpora.

Really in initial and medial position have already been dealt with in detail by, for example, Greenbaum 1969, Bolinger 1972, Quirk *et al.* 1972 and Jacobson 1978, but, to my knowledge, very little has been said about *really* in final position where its function seems to be even more doubtful. Since this position was common in the data, especially in the conversations, I shall give a brief overview of the occurrences and make a few suggestions as to function.

7.5 *Really* IN POST-POSITION

To be able to compare written and spoken output, I take the clause as a term of reference. The term post-position indicates either that *really* is placed in clause-final position:

(4) I'm English really, Diana though   P 11 148

or that it is placed after a potential head but is not clause-final:

(5) it /didn't make any DÌFFERENCE// /RÈALLY// to the result
     of the EXAMINÀTION//   1.1:1051

A: clause-final

In the LOB sample, *really* occurred twice at the end of a clause, both renderings of direct speech, and in the LLC sample twenty-two times. This seemed to indicate that *really* in final position is typical of speech. In order to get a more reliable idea of the difference in distribution, I looked at the LOB and LLC (reduced version) corpora. The result is displayed in Table 7.3. As

Table 7.3 *Really* in clause-final position in LOB and LLC

	Punctuation		Prosody			Total	% of all
	After comma	No comma	Sep TU	Sep TU after pause	No sep TU		313/539 LOB/LLC
LOB	3	10				13	4.2
LLC			30	2	57	89	16.5

appears, clause-final position was much more common in the spoken than in the written data: 16 per cent vs. 4 per cent. Notice that 'end of clause' corresponds to 'end of tone unit'. In LOB, *really* was separated from the rest of the clause in a few cases:

(6) She lost either way, really.   P 06 143

which should indicate that *really* is an evaluater, expressing the writer's attitude to the preceding proposition. The separation by comma would probably correspond to a pause in the spoken discourse:

(7) we :don't know 'what it MÉANS//—/RÉALLY//   3.5:281

or perhaps just intonation contours with *really* in a separate tone unit:

(8) it's /ăL'most//—/THRÈE 'weeks// /RĚALLY//   2.7:862

depending on the degree of emphasis *really* in that position is supposed to convey.

An interesting variant that occurred only in LLC is hidden in the figure under 'no separate tone unit', 57, and consists of *really* in clause-final position followed by a comment clause, is 'I think', 'I suppose', 'you know', etc. Such clauses were characteristically uttered within the same tone unit as *really*:

(9) which is /QUÌTE re'vealing RÉALLY I think//   2.9:333

Quirk *et al.* (1972: 734) define comment clauses as disjuncts which express 'the speaker's attitude to the main clause, or his manner of asserting it', adding that they generally occur in a separate tone unit.

Comment clauses are undeniably speech-specific, a product of the conversational situation, and serve as a communicative cue to the hearer in the same way as a tag would do in a similar position. Faerch and Kasper 1982 use the term 'cajoler' whose basic function, they say, is interpersonal. Referring to Edmondson and House 1981, they state that cajolers serve to 'establish, increase, or indeed restore harmony between the two conversational partners'. Crystal and Davy 1975 define 'softeners' in much the same way, although they emphasize the stylistic function.

Really in final position, it seems, often has this softening or cajoling effect, but with the modification that it is slightly more personal and message-oriented, whereas, for example, 'you know' is explicitly appealing and inherently interpersonal.

B: post-head

In this position *really* separates a clause constituent from the rest of the clause and is consequently not clause-final. The constituent to the right is either obligatory, as in the only instance in the written data:

(10) So I'd only need, really, to begin: "Isn't . . .   K 10 175

or optional in the clause structure:

(11) it /doesn't BÒTHER 'me RÉALLY// at/AÌLL//   1.12:506

The spoken data contained 29 instances of *really* placed in this position, always at the end of a tone unit.

Post-head position was particularly common with extraposition, where the two parts separated by *really* were connected by copular BE:

(12) it /is a PRÒBLEM really// how to !TEACH this STUFF//   1.9:1128

and between the head and an optional postmodifier:

(13) I've /no in'tention NÒW of//—/now of . of
     :publishing :ÀRTICLES RÉALLY// /from . from the BÒOK//   3.6:436

where there is a characteristic 'I mean' relation between the head and its postmodifier.

Table 7.4 shows the distribution of intonation contours for *really* in clause-final and post-head position. Except in the 13 cases where *really* was followed by a comment clause it always occurred at end of tone unit. Rising or falling–rising intonation dominated in both positions followed by cases where *really* did not carry nucleus. Falling tone was rare and level tone occurred only once.

Table 7.4 Intonation contours of *really* in clause-final and post-head position

	(Fall)Rise	Fall	Level	Ø	Total
Clause-final	66	6	1	16	88
Post-head	12	2	—	9	30

Placed in post-position, *really* typically constituted the second part of a pitch sequence consisting of fall on the last nuclear element of the clause proper and rise or fall–rise on *really*. In those cases where a comment clause constituted the end of the utterance, this clause did not have a nucleus but continued the main pitch contour.

There were exceptions. One was illustrated in (11). Greenbaum (1969: 127, 183) discusses examples where *naturally* and *really* occur in a separate tone unit, *naturally* in final position and *really* in post-head position, both echoing the immediately preceding nucleus in terms of intensifier/disjunct function. He comes to the conclusion that the separation in an independent tone unit is not in itself sufficient to identify a disjunct; also, in the case of *really*, that it can still be an intensifier since it echoes the preceding nucleus.

Really in clause-final and post-head position varied from prosodically unmarked to marked both by tone unit boundaries and nucleus and by pauses. Consider the following, most contrasting cases of *really* in clause-final position:

(14) Clause-final
(a) I've been working pretty :HÀRD 'really//   2.7:856

(b) it's /not so ¹easy as . you THÌNK RÉALLY// 1.5:1118
(c) it's /really for you to DECÎDE// /RÉALLY// 2.2:25
(d) I don't know if anything's TĚRRIBLY new at !ÀLL// . /RÉALLY// 2.7:437

It is tempting to regard *really* which is separated from the rest of the clause as an evaluater reflecting the speaker's attitude to what he is saying, wherever it is placed in the utterance, and *really* with no separating features as an intensifier emphasizing an element of clause, regardless of whether it is placed before or after the head. It is also tempting to take mobility as a criterion of evaluater function.

Unfortunately, this is being too categorical. Not only must the combined effect of position and prosody be considered, but also the wider context. The most reliable way, however, would be to test a number of utterances with native informants. Lacking such tests at this point, I will only very tentatively suggest possible functions of *really* in post-position.

In none of the examples under (14) does it seem natural to move *really* to initial position, which should indicate intensifier function (cf. Quirk *et al.* 1972: 441). If *really* were to be moved at all, the most natural place would be after operator/NEG (cf. (14c)). But as it stands, *really* does seem to reflect the speaker's view on the entire proposition, only with varying intensity from really// in (a) to /RÉALLY// in (d). In (a) the effect resembled that of a softener, for example, 'you see'; in (d) the effect is that of an afterthought, possible to paraphrase 'on second thoughts'.

(15) Post-head
(a) and it's IMPǑRTANT ¹really// for somebody that has
more experience 2.9:1233
(b) but it's very im:portant RĚALLY// . in many WAYS to
¹write 2.9:1266
(c) just not INTERESTED e¹nough// . /RĚALLY// to do that 3.1:135
(d) EŃOUGH for me as it ìs I think// /RÉALLY// . in LÒTS of
WÁYS// 1.9:789

The main difference between *really* in clause-final and post-head position seems to be that it acts more as an evaluater in the first set, with the entire preceding proposition as its scope, and more like an intensifier in the second set, where the nuclear element immediately preceding *really* is focalized and gets special emphasis.

It is still an open question why *really* occurs finally at all instead of inside the clause. The answer nearest at hand is that this is a reflection of the speaker's ongoing planning strategy. He may realize, at that very point, that he wants to modify what he is saying, either by softening an assertion, or by giving more emphasis, or by adding an afterthought. There is also the possibility that *really* in post-position has become entirely void of meaning and rather reflects mannerism than a conscious speaker strategy.

7.6 SPEECH-SPECIFIC FUNCTIONS

The following functions of *really* are never met with in written language other than in printed dialogue. There were no instances in LOB.

A REOPENER
B CONTINUER
C PLANNER

They are all products of, and bound to the communicative situation of spoken discourse. Reopeners and continuers constitute the hearer's response to the current speaker's output but with different effects; the reopener affects the turn-taking system and results in speaker-shift, the continuer encourages the speaker to hold his turn. Planners are overt manifestations of the speaker's ongoing planning strategy and have a turn-holding effect.

A *Really* as a reopener

A reopener is a move in the interaction which, by eliciting confirmation, reopens an exchange which would otherwise have been terminated (cf. Stubbs 1981). Reopeners are often realized by tags, such as 'did he' or 'aren't you' and also by phrases involving *really*, for example, 'did he really get there', but *really* in isolation, indicating surprise or incredulity, may have the same eliciting effect.

A reopener is either the hearer's reaction to an informing move:

(16) B: . . . and THÀT was//
     you /KNÓW//
     in times that Ì can re'member// ,
   A: +/RÉALLY//+
   a: +good+ Lord
   B: /oh YÊS//
   A: /YÈS//   2.3:34

or it is the questioner's reaction to the response:

(17) A: /Oscar is GŎING to the States//
   B: ((/WÈLL)) this is what I ''/HÈARD//
     just be/fore I came A!wĂY// —
   A: /RÊALLY//
   B: ((/YÈS//)) —   1.2:349

Informing moves, as in (16), are generally followed by a supporting move, such as 'yeah' or 'I see', indicating that the hearer has received the information (cf. Coulthard and Montgomery 1981), but in this case the hearer queries the truth of the message, and *really* serves as a request for confirmation.

Q/R exchanges, as in (17), are usually terminated by a follow-up move which indicates that the questioner accepts the response; the normal sequence is thus Q R F (see further Berry 1981; Coulthard and Brazil 1981; Stenström 1982).

The normal pitch contour for *really* as a reopener is fall–rise or rise. The fact that *really* in (17) with rising–falling tone functions as a reopener is probably an effect of the long pause after the response. An exchange that seemed to be terminated by the response is suddenly reopened by *really*, uttered by A after some consideration, as if he were not quite convinced. A contributory factor may be that *really* in itself is not just an empty word but retains some of its original meaning and therefore serves to check the truth/falsity of the preceding utterance when occurring in this particular position.

B *Really* as a continuer

Whereas the reopener signals surprise and doubt, the continuer is more or less neutral, to the effect that the continuer does not invite a confirming response; the current speaker continues and there is consequently no speaker-shift. Compare (17) and (18):

(18) B: I /don't know if he DRÒPPED that//
      A: /oh RÊALLY//
      B: cos . well /I /I don't KNÒW//
          +/when he was trying to FÌND+ ...   1.5:257

Contrary to what was the case in (17), the current speaker does not pay attention to the insertion of *really* but goes on speaking.

The term 'continuer' is taken over from Schegloff 1982. He uses it for items by which the hearer claims, rather than shows, understanding and/or attention and by which he indicates that he understands that the current speaker intends to continue speaking, by passing on the opportunity of taking over the turn. He does not include *really* among the continuers but refers to it as a 'reaction' which may be invited by the immediately preceding talk, 'aside from or instead of or in addition to' the continuer. According to the present data, however, *really* acts in the same way as *uh huh*, which is Schegloff's example.

Faerch and Kasper 1982, referring to Edmondson 1977, use the term 'uptaking' which in their definition signals to the present speaker that 'the channel is still open and that the speaker's message is being taken in' and also serves to reinforce the current distribution of discourse roles.

The typical tone of *really* functioning as a continuer is falling or rising–falling. Rising tone occurred in a couple of cases and did seem to indicate surprise rather than acceptance of information and passing on the opportunity of taking over. As illustrated in (19), such cases are ambiguous:

(19) B: ... and pre/sumably he's got something equally FÀTAL//
      /or perhaps it ìs lung cancer//

A: /RÉALLY//
B: /this is all very sÀD//
  I /feel . bÀD about ((that))//   1.4.1042

The analysis of *really* as a continuer or as a re-opener depends on the way the 'current' speaker's utterance is interpreted. 'this is all very sad' might just as well be seen as a confirmation of a comment that the speaker would have added anyway. In the first case *really* would have been analysed as a reopener, in the second as a continuer.

C *Really* as a planner

This is a highly tentative category where *really* is seen as a device in the speaker's ongoing planning process. I have provisionally identified three subcategories—projecter, react and filler—with the characteristics as shown in Table 7.5. Reacts, projecters and fillers are alike in most respects; they typically occur at the beginning of an utterance where the speaker has not yet made up his mind how to proceed, they occur with repetitions, hesitators and softeners, and are typically followed by a new start, that is, a syntactic reformulation.

Table 7.5 Characteristics of planners

	Beginning	Repetition	Hesitation	New Start	Softener	Nucleus	Pro/ retrospect
React	+	+	+	+	+	+	+
Projecter	±	+	+	+	+	±	+
Filler	+	+	+	+	+	−	−

Functioning as a filler, *really* differs from reacts and projecters in that it does not generally have a nucleus and is not oriented towards the preceding utterance or towards an element that follows in the same utterance. Reacts, on the other hand, always carry a nucleus; projecters sometimes do and sometimes do not. Reacts may be oriented towards the preceding speaker's utterance or towards the speaker's own utterance, whereas projecters point forward.

The planner function is most obvious in the projecter. I noticed when I looked at the data that *really* in certain positions, as illustrated in (20), seemed to point forward to a head later on in the utterance and that it was therefore different from items that have been classified as fillers, that is, items which occur outside the syntactic structure of an utterance. According to Brown 1977, the principal duty of a filler is to 'fill the silence and maintain the speaker's right to speak, while he organizes what he wants to say'. Planners are different and can partly be described in syntactic terms, it seems either as intensifiers or evaluaters. Consider (20):

(20) and /I . /I get !really [əm] - - ((you know)) when ! [?] when
     I'm 'trying to còoκ// . and /people come and CHẤT// I /I
     get !terribly put òFF//   2.7:69

The following features co-occur:

o   *really* is preceded by hesitation (here realized by repetition)
    I I get
o   *really* is followed by a new start
    and I I get (repeated later by *I get*)
o   *really* collocates with a filler in combination with a pause and a hesitator
    [əm] - - *you know*
o   *really* does not carry a nucleus

As is pointed out by Brown 1977, repetitions, hesitations, reformulations and fillers such as *well* and *I think* typically appear at the beginning of an utterance while the 'meat of the utterance' is not arrived at until the end, when the speaker has worked out what he wants to say. My suggestion is that *really* is part of the planning process and that it anticipates a head, here realized by *put off*; that this is so seems to be confirmed by the fact that it is replaced in front of the head by the intensifier *terribly*. In anticipating a head, *really* can consequently be described as a 'dangling' intensifier. At the same time, it attracts the hearer's attention to the fact that there is more to come; therefore it also acts as a turn-holder.

Judging by these data, *really* in the planning function is also met with in the middle of an utterance, that is, when the speaker suddenly loses the thread or makes a momentary stop for reconsideration:

(21) and /ALL this was DÓNE [ə:] // - - /by - - kind of letting - [ə:] - - . /
     {WÈLL} RĔALLY by 'just [ə:] - - 'sort of [ə]// - /starting from
     :NÒTHING//   2.3:115

He probably knows, already from the start, what he wants to say but not exactly how to put it in words. Notice the combination of fillers, pauses and hesitators that intervene before the message is delivered and the utterance is completed.

There is also the case where *really* in an independent tone unit serves as a react and is similar to an evaluater at the syntactic level:

(22) d: you're you're an awkward customer aren't you
        A: (- - - laughs) -[ə:m] - - - /{WÈLL} 'O!Ḱ//
        /RĔALLY// - I /mean - - -   2.4:814

Really seems to signal a strong objection to the previous speaker's statement. There were only two other cases likely to be referred to this category.

The filler function, finally, may be illustrated by (23), where *really* occurs in the middle of a long utterance:

(23) .... but /really I've got about . :THRÈE WÉEKS "less than that of
/hardish :wŏRK//   1.1:55

and where it can hardly be described in syntactic terms at all but is outside the syntactic structure of the utterance.

7.7 CONCLUDING REMARKS

What *really* does in the discourse is strongly related to its position, both within an utterance and in a sequence of interaction.

One feature that the written and spoken data had in common was the position of *really* immediately after NEG. Assuming that this use has a softening effect on the negative statement, one might have expected it to be much more frequent in speech, where the speaker is confronted with his hearer, than in writing, where no second party is present. It is therefore likely that more extensive data would yield a different result.

What finally decides the function of *really* in speech is the combined effect of position and prosody, always in relation to the wider context. This implies that the exact function is extremely difficult to determine, all the more as sufficient knowledge of the wider context is often missing. Post-position, clause-final and especially post-head, which was found to be characteristic of speech, was suggested to reflect the speaker's ongoing planning process. As to the functions of *really* in the so-called speech-specific category, my suggestions were highly tentative. More comprehensive studies of spoken data would therefore be helpful.

I hope to have given at least some useful indications of what *really* really does and invite further suggestions.

KEY TO PROSODIC AND PARALINGUISTIC SYMBOLS

/	onset
//	end of tone unit
{ }	subordinate tone unit
[ ]	word partials
(( ))	not clear
. -	short and long pauses
+ +	simultaneous speech
:	higher pitch level than preceding syllable
!	higher pitch level than preceding pitch prominent syllable
' "	normal and heavy stresses
´	rise
`	fall
ˇ	fall–rise
^	rise–fall
-	level

8 Discourse structure and interpretive strategies in adult–child talk: some properties of 'summons–answer' sequences

Margaret MacLure
The University of East Anglia

8.1 INTRODUCTION: 'CONVERSATIONS' BETWEEN ADULTS AND INFANTS

Children are born into a social world where, right from the start, their behaviour is interpreted as 'meaningful' by those who take care of them. Parents and other adults make sense—literally—of infants' cries, yawns, burps, smiles etc., not just as clues to their state of material well-being, but also as communicative acts. Moreover, one of the major achievements of such interpretive strategies is to confer upon babies' behaviours not just the semblance of intentionality, but of being elements of coordinated conversation. Kaye and Charney, for instance, observe that 'In the early months, whenever an infant gives his mother any behaviour that can be interpreted as if he had taken a turn in conversation, it will be; and if he does not, she often pretends that he has' (1981: 47). Recognizing this pervasive practice by adults of constructing conversations round babies' actions, several analysts have emphasized its developmental significance: by continuously treating babies' behaviours as communicatively intended contributions to conversations, adults provide children with a foothold on the world of shared meanings, and the communally owned code for conveying these.[1]

Snow 1977 has examined in detail some of the ways in which mothers exploit the mechanism of discourse structuring to orchestrate 'conversations' with babies as young as 3 and 7 months, and it will be worth mentioning these briefly, as I shall argue later that some of the strategies she identified are similar to, or can be seen as precursors of, conversational strategies used by adults in interaction with older children. A first set of strategies identified by Snow operates RETROSPECTIVELY, by conferring a conversational significance and turn-status upon the child's behaviour after it has occurred. One very effective means of doing this is to exploit the adjacency-pairing mechanism for turn allocation (Sacks, Schegloff and Jefferson 1974) by responding to specific behaviours by the child as if they were first parts of adjacency pairs. A vocalization, for instance, can be constituted after the fact as a 'greeting' by receiving a greeting in response; a cry can be responded to as if it were a 'protest' (Snow 1977: 17).[2] Other strategies operate PROSPECTIVELY, that is, they assign to babies' next actions the status of a 'response' to an initiation by the adult. For instance, by designing a question around normal expectations of what a baby is likely to do in a particular situation, adults can confer on that behaviour the appearance of an answer. Snow gives the following example:

(1) Mother:
     Are you finished?
     Yes? (removing bottle)
     Well was that nice? [Snow 1977: 14]

where the initial question is designed around expectations of what a baby is likely to do when her bottle is removed: she will either cry or not. Whichever 'response' in fact occurs, it can be seen as an 'answer' to the question: crying would mean *no*; not crying, *yes*. Snow discusses several other devices for constructing conversations—for instance, taking BOTH turns in an exchange, by answering questions on the baby's behalf—but the examples discussed above exemplify certain general aspects of adults' sense-making procedures which apply on most occasions of interacting with young babies, and it is these general characteristics which will be of relevance to the analysis of conversations involving older children presented below. These are: firstly, that much if not all of the responsibility for creating the semblance of conversations is shouldered by the adult. Secondly, that notwithstanding this (or rather precisely because of this), the infant's behaviour takes on the appearance of being reciprocally related to the adult's turns at talk. Thirdly, that the means by which this is achieved rely on adults exploiting the mechanisms of conversational structuring in describable ways. Fourthly and finally, that the creation of recognizable conversational sequences is achieved by the design and positioning of adult utterances around the child's preceding, ongoing or anticipated actions, and is closely synchronized with these.

In the remainder of the chapter I shall discuss some properties of conversations between adults and older children, aged between 18 and 36 months,[3] focusing on one particular sequential environment: that of sequences initiated by a 'summons' from the child. I shall try to show how adults continue to play an interpretive and supportive role in interaction with older children by adopting strategies designed to get talk started and to ensure collaboration over a discourse topic when some interactional 'problem' arises following the summons. I shall also suggest that the syntactic form of the adults' 'repair' utterances in these environments is associated with the interactional ends these are designed to achieve.

8.2 GETTING TALK STARTED: SUMMONS–ANSWER SEQUENCES[4]

One of the prerequisites to getting talk started is the requirement for the intending initiator to secure her addressee's 'availability for talk' (Schegloff 1968), and on some occasions speakers may explicitly attempt to secure this by a prefatory utterance to which the addressee is expected to respond, before the first speaker proceeds with the utterance in mind (see e.g. Schegloff 1968; Keenan and Schieffelin 1976; Ochs, Schieffelin and Platt 1979). In Schegloff's (1968) terms, a first speaker may issue a summons, to which the addressee is required to give an answer. Summonses in inter-adult talk frequently take the form of vocatives, and answers to vocative summonses usually have the form of a simple interrogative particle such as *what? mm? yes?*

Before going on to look at sequences beginning with a summons–answer (hereafter 's–a') pair in adult–child conversation, I shall briefly mention some properties of successfully accomplished s–a sequences. Schegloff 1968 suggests that the s–a pair is one method by which participants achieve 'coordinated entry' into talk, by extracting mutual obligations to continue on completion of the s–a component—the first step in that continuation being the right and responsibility of the summoner. The summoner, in other words, by issuing the summons, incurs the obligation to talk again following the answer; and, reciprocally, the answerer both 'commits himself to staying with the encounter' (p. 1083) and, by virtue of the interrogative form of the answer, hands the floor back to the summoner to continue in the next turn. This gives rise to two properties of s–a pairs: firstly, they are 'non-terminal'—that is, a conversation cannot properly end with an s–a pair. Secondly, s–a sequences display an 'aba' structure of three alternating turns. A further property of s–a sequences noted by Schegloff is the 'non-repeatability' of summonses after answers: once the summons has been repeated, it is not in order for the summoner to issue a further summons (to the same person)—though of course when the summons is not answered further attempts are in order.

Turning now to s–a sequences in the data under consideration here: there were many examples of 'successful' s–a sequences, exemplifying the three-turn pattern described above. However, particularly in the earlier recordings (18–27 months), there were a considerable number of child-initiated s–a sequences which deviated in various ways from this sequential patterning, as a result of some interactional 'problem' arising at the third-turn point in the sequence: that is, the point at which the child, having issued a summons and received an answer, failed to produce a recognizable continuation in the next turn. This interactional failure consisted, variously, in: (a) failure to continue at all (violating the constraint on 'non-terminality'); (b) repetition (or reformulation) of the original summons (violating the constraint on 'non-repeatability'); (c) an uninterpretable continuation. Examples of each of these conditions will be given below. Following this interactional problem at third-turn point, adults typically attempted to 'repair' the potential conversational breakdown, and it is these repair devices that I shall discuss below, suggesting that the repair utterances display recurrent syntactic properties which are associated both with the nature of the original summons, and with the sequential placement of the repair utterance itself.

Consider first the following examples, where the child at third-turn point repeats the initial (vocative) summons.[5] (See Appendix for conventions of transcription.)

(2) Debbie—R3S01: 1 month
    C: ooh ooh (high-pitched)
    (.)
— mummy
    M: what?
— C: mummy:
    M: [what d'you want?
    C: mummy (.) /bʊbʊ/ (indecipherable)

(3) Geoffrey—R4S20: 24 months
— C: mummy
    M: what?
— C: mummy
    M: what did you do?

A first point to note about these examples is the relationship between the adult's first and second utterance. In each example the original vocative summons receives the expected 'minimal' answer (*what?*), while the repeated summons receives a full wh-question. Moreover, the wh-question in each case relates to some possible concern of the CHILD's. This shift from single item interrogative to wh-question following the repeated summons can be seen as an attempt to propose a continuation on the child's behalf, when she has failed to recognizably take up this opportunity at the expected third-turn point. As Schegloff 1968 notes, the 'minimalness' of single-item answers allows the topic of talk to remain undefined until the third-turn point, thus respecting the summoner's right to talk on some topic of concern to him. For unlike other question-type utterances, single-item interrogatives do not display preconceptions or predispositions on the part of the speaker as to what sort of answer is anticipated. In contrast, wh-questions, though more open-ended than yes/no questions (see below), nevertheless display some orientation on the part of the questioner to the general area in which an answer is likely to lie. Keenan and Schieffelin 1976, for example, argue that wh-questions such as *what do you want?* or *what's the matter?* propose as discourse topics their primary presuppositions 'you want something', 'something is the matter'. In examples such as (2) and (3) above, therefore, the adult's second utterance can be seen as an attempt to propose a discourse topic when the child has failed to offer this on her own account at the expected third-turn point.

    The examples above contain vocative summonses. However, there are other ways of attempting to secure the attention and participation of a listener. Children may, for example, solicit the listener's attention by means of cries, squeals, shouts or other indicators of distress, effort or excitement (cf. Keenan and Schieffelin 1976; McTear 1981); for example:

(4) Neil—R4S08: 24 months
    C: aaah! (shouting)
    M: what's the matter?

C: *bike (.) bike
M: go and get your bike then.

One notable feature of such summonses is that they almost always elicit *non-minimal* answers from adults. As in the above example, the adult's answer is often in wh-form, and is therefore less 'neutral' with respect to a possible discourse topic at third-turn point than single-item answers.

But note that summonses in the form of distressed noises or 'effortful' vocalizations themselves suggest more about the summoner's possible interests and motivations in initiating talk than do vocatives (unless accompanied by marked tone of voice, intonation contour or facial expression). The former suggest not only that the summoner wants to engage the addressee's participation, but that she may be doing it for a purpose which is partly retrievable from the nature of the summons itself. So crying, for example, may be interpreted by the listener as suggesting that something is 'wrong', or 'the matter' etc. In contrast to s–a sequences initiated by vocative, therefore, in sequences such as these summoner and answerer begin to collaborate on the topic during the s–a pair itself.

The same observation may be made of summonses which take the form of conventionalized expressions of discomfort, pain, surprise etc., such as *ouch*! *damn*! *wow*! and so on. These also typically elicit wh-questions as answers. However, in adult–child talk answers to summonses of this type may also be accompanied by a prefatory reciprocal 'noticing' item which mirrors the child's original exclamation (cf. Schegloff, reported in Keenan and Schieffelin 1976; also Bloom 1973: 108):

(5) Neil—R4S01: 24 months
     Neil is playing with his grandmother's make-up
→   C: oh dear
→   GM oh dear (.) what have you done?
     C: *
     GM: [dropped it on the ground?
     C: yeah

Non-vocative summonses such as crying, grunting etc., and conventionalized expressive noises such as *oh dear*, therefore, usually elicit wh-questions as answers. In this they are similar to the REPAIR strategies following repeated vocative summonses as discussed above, in that they propose topics centring round some concern of the child's. While wh-questions in both of these environments partly delimit the possible topic for the child's next turn, they still accord the child a fair amount of conversational latitude in further specifying the topic in her next turn: many different things can be 'the matter', 'wanted' etc. The interactional initiative therefore remains largely with the child as initiator of the sequence to specify what will be talked about in the next turn.

However, it sometimes happens that an interactional problem arises following the wh-question—in both of these environments—and when this

happens the adult may attempt to repair the sequence by continuing with a
yes/no question, as in the following:

(6) Geoffrey—R2S02: 21 months
     C and M are playing with plastic cups
     C: (squeals)
     M: now what's the matter?
     C: mm
→   M: d'you want it back?
     C: (screams)

     .
     .

(7) Debbie—R3S22: 21 months[6]
     C: ah- ah (.) mummy
     M: what's the matter darling?
     C: * * *
→   M: did you bang your head?
           (1.1)
         oh dear

In these examples, and also (5) above, when C's utterance at third-turn
position fails to offer a recognizable on-topic continuation following M's wh-
question, M continues in her next turn with a yes/no question. This can also
be seen in the vocative-initiated sequence (8) below, where the adult's
utterances are progressively 'upgraded' from single-item interrogative
(*what?*), to wh-question, to yes/no question:

(8) C: daddy
→   F: what?
     C: daddy
→   F: what've you done?
→   broken a toy?
            (1.2)
          eh?
            (0.8)
        little scamp
     C: laughs

(In this example, however, F does not allow C time to produce an answer to
the wh-question before proceeding with the yes/no question: see MacLure
1981 for a fuller discussion of this and similar examples.)

   In each of the examples (5)–(8), the adult reformulates (cf. Ervin-Tripp and
Miller 1977; Snow 1977; French and MacLure 1979) the original wh-question
as a yes/no question. By doing this, the adult attempts to specify FURTHER a
topic on behalf of the child, by further delimiting the topic area introduced in
the wh-question. Consequently, the yes/no questions work to reduce the
cognitive and interactional demands on the child as co-participant: instead of
requiring her to select one from an open-ended set of possible answers, as is

the case with wh-questions, the yes/no questions require only acceptance or rejection of a proposition which is already expressed in the question itself.[7]

We can note further that the yes/no question in examples such as these, like the wh-question which preceded it, relates to some concern of the child's. For instance, in (7) M characterizes the 'matter' introduced in the prior wh-question as being, possibly, the fact that C had banged her head. In (5), GM offers as a possible answer to *what have you done*? that C had 'dropped it on the ground'. The candidate interpretations which these yes/no questions offer are therefore tailored to the child's ongoing/just-completed activity: that is, they offer an interpretation of some observable state of affairs which the child is involved in—and which she may therefore have had an intention to communicate. In these instances ((5) and (7)) the adult's yes/no question characterizes the child's so-far-undeclared intention as having been to offer some sort of INFORMING utterance. In other instances (e.g (6)), the yes/no question proposes a possible 'want' on the part of the child: in other words, it offers an interpretation of the child's initial summons as a preface to a REQUEST. Looking back to the examples from Snow's (1977) analysis of mother–infant interaction referred to in my Introduction, we can see that the yes/no questions under discussion here bear some similarity to those early sense-making procedures, in that they offer as topics for talk propositions built around the child's current actions or preoccupations.

It sometimes happens that even the yes/no question in s–a sequences fails to secure an appropriate response—and hence collaboration over a discourse topic—from the child. And when this happens adults frequently take further steps to establish a topic: for instance, they may repeat the yes/no question, possibly in expanded form, or via a 'prompting' reinitiation such as *eh*? (cf. (8) above). But in the absence of a recognizable response to the yes/no question—either after its first occurrence or following one or more attempted reinitiations—adults may resort to a further and final strategy which terminates the sequence with an utterance implying that the child HAD produced such a response, when in fact none had occurred. For instance in (7), Debbie's mother's last utterance—*oh dear*—implies that a positive response had been given to the prior yes/no question (*did you bang your head*?). And in (8), Neil's father's final utterance *little scamp* implies that Neil had confirmed that he's 'broken a toy'. Again, we can see a similarity between these strategies, which retrospectively confer answering status on the child's behalf, and those examples from Snow 1977 referred to at the outset.

In 'acknowledging' a fictitious response to a preceding yes/no question, adults are exploiting a mechanism of conversational structuring associated with the asking and answering of questions. As many analysts have observed (e.g. Sinclair and Coulthard 1975; Mehan 1978; Drew 1981), question sequences are often done in a 'three part' format:

A: question		*A: what's the matter
B: answer	e.g.:	B: I banged my head
A: 'follow up'		A: oh dear

where, following B's answer, A may do a further turn devoted to acknow-ledging or evaluating the answer. Because of the three-part structure associated with question sequences, the adult's 'acknowledgment' subse-quent to the unanswered yes/no question in examples such as those above can be heard as acknowledging an ANSWER.

If we compare the different types of adult utterances which have been discussed, we can see that there is a hierarchical ordering amongst them in terms of how far they define the topic on the child's behalf, and consequently in terms of the interactional demands that they place on the child as co-participant. Considering these utterance types in comparison with one another, and in increasing order of topic-specification, these were:

1. minimal interrogative   —   e.g. 'what?' (in answer to vocatives)
2. wh-question   —   e.g. 'what's the matter?'
3. yes/no question   —   e.g. 'did you bang your head?'
4. 'follow-up'   —   e.g. 'oh dear'

8.3 SUMMARY AND CONCLUSION

In the foregoing discussion, I have tried to show, firstly, how adults attempt to remedy interactional breakdown and secure 'coordinated entry' when children fail to offer comprehensible discourse topics on their own behalf, following an apparent 'summons' to engage in talk. The various types of interrogative repair utterances can be seen as attempts to 'make sense' of children's initial attention-seeking utterances and vocalizations by searching for a possible communicative motive underlying their production. Thus the repair utterances propose, with varying degrees of specificity, topics centring round some possible event or state of affairs in which the child appears to be involved, and which she may therefore have intended to communicate. I have also tried to show that the syntactic form of these topic-proposing questions is not in free variation, but is associated both with the nature of the initial summons (i.e. whether it is vocative or otherwise), and with the sequential positioning of the repair utterance (i.e. whether it is a first or subsequent attempt at repair). I have suggested further that the sequential ordering of repair types within sequences—that is, minimal interrogative–wh-question–yes/no question–follow up—is in turn bound up with adults' efforts to sustain the talk by proposing discourse topics while AT THE SAME TIME trying to avoid trespassing on the child's interactional right and obligation as summoner to do this on her own behalf. The repair utterances therefore get progressively 'upgraded' in terms of their propositional specificity in line with diagnoses of continuing interactional problems on the child's part.

In presenting this (partial) analysis of child-initiated s–a sequences I have also tried to exemplify a method of looking at conversations between adults and children which attends to the interpretive effort which adults put into sustaining conversations with children. In all of the examples discussed we can see adults trying—amongst other things—to make sense of their children's initial utterances and vocalizations as prefaces to communicative acts; scanning their behaviour for the material out of which to construct topics for talk; diagnosing interactional problems and designing their own utterances to overcome these. This interpretive, supportive and remedial work shows certain similarities to the conversation-building strategies used by adults in interaction with young babies which were referred to in my Introduction—despite the fact that the children in this study have undoubtedly reached a point where they are capable of conveying communicative intentions in their own right, rather than being agents in the communication process only by proxy, through the intervention of others.

NOTES

1. See, for example, Wolff 1968; Ryan 1974; Bruner 1975; Newson and Newson 1975; Trevarthen, Hubley and Sheeran 1975; Edwards 1978; Lock 1978; Shotter 1978; Dore 1979.
2. Adjacency-pair types identified include: questions and answers; compliments and acceptances/rejections (Pomerantz 1978); greetings and greetings responses; requests and grantings/rejections (Garvey 1975; Wootton forthcoming); summonses and answers (Schegloff 1968: see section 8.2).
3. The examples discussed are drawn from a corpus of audio recordings collected during an SSRC-funded longitudinal project, 'Language Development in Pre-School Children', carried out in the School of Education at the University of Bristol between 1972 and 1978, under the directorship of C. G. Wells. For a fuller description of the methodology and data collection procedures used, see Wells (1981: Introduction).
4. The arguments developed in this chapter are based on research presented in a doctoral dissertation, 'Making Sense of Children's Talk: Structure and Strategy in Adult–Child Conversation' (University of York, 1981).
5. For reasons of space, reference can be made in this chapter only to relatively few examples from the audio-recorded data. These should therefore be treated as exemplars of a larger corpus of examples. Chapters 4 and 5 of the dissertation cited in note 4 above present an extended discussion of issues raised here, with additional examples.
6. Sequences such as these, where a vocative summons either follows or accompanies a non-vocative vocalization (crying, shouting etc.) are usually answered, as here, in wh-question form.
7. French and MacLure 1979 identify a similar sequential ordering of question types in talk between teachers and infant-school pupils.

APPENDIX

Conventions and layout of transcribed examples

Speakers' contributions are arranged vertically. Abbreviations for identifying speakers are as follows:

C — child
M — mother

F — father
GM— grandmother
GF— grandfather
A — other adult
MM—Margaret MacLure

Contextual information relating to participants' non-verbal behaviour and to the physical context of utterances is enclosed in parentheses: (²).

Tentative interpretations of utterances or parts of utterances are enclosed in angle brackets: ⟨ ⟩. Where two possible interpretations are offered, these are separated by an oblique stroke; for example: ⟨daddy/doggy.

Indecipherable utterances are indicated by asterisks. Number of asterisks corresponds to number of syllables identified in the utterance.

Symbols of the International Phonetic Alphabet, enclosed in oblique strokes, are used occasionally to transcribe utterances over which there is some uncertainty. Elsewhere speech is transcribed according to Standard English orthography.

Other symbols used are as follows:

[	indicates overlap of speaker's turns. Bracket is placed at point at which overlap begins.
:	placed after a syllable indicates noticeable lengthening.
↑	before an utterance or part of utterance indicates a shift of pitch relatively higher than that which is normal for the speaker.
-	(hyphen) indicates a hiatus or 'cut off' in delivery, for instance at point of interruption by another speaker or prior to a self-correction.
(1.2)	indicates a pause (here of 1.2 seconds), either within or between utterances. Pauses over 0.5 seconds are measured in tenths of a second.
(.)	indicates a pause of 0.5 seconds or less
→	before utterances within examples, indicates part(s) of a sequence to which discussion in the text particularly refers.
.	indicates that part of the sequence has been omitted.
.	
.	
*	placed immediately before an example, and in the absence of an identification number, an asterisk indicates that the example has been constructed by the analyst for purposes of exposition.

9 Modelling discourse participants' knowledge

Gillian Brown
University of Essex

This chapter stems from a rather different mode of enquiry into discourse processes than that of many of the other papers at the Hatfield Discourse Conference (where this work was first presented).[1] Many of them worked within the framework of conversational analysis, an analysis which is particularly concerned with what Stephen Levinson has described as being that conversational structure 'which is now known to have its own elaborate architecture' where 'the functions that utterances perform are in large part due to the place they have within specific conversational sequences' (Levinson 1980).

The type of analysis which I want to describe here leans more on work in psycholinguistics and artificial intelligence than on work in sociolinguistics. However, I hope it may be seen as complementary to work done within the framework of conversational analysis, rather than, in any sense, as competitive with it. In my view we are all struggling with different parts of the anatomy of discourse, and any mode of approach which sheds light on how we participate in interaction, how we understand what we say to each other, how we understand what we encounter as written texts, is to be welcomed. If the blind man beside me will tell me how the trunk of the elephant feels to him, I, equally blind, shall in return tell him how the tail of the elephant feels to me.

In this chapter I shall be particularly concerned with that aspect of language which is primarily concerned with the transference of information—sometimes called the IDEATIONAL /PROPOSITIONAL/COGNITIVE function. I am concerned with how participants in an interaction may package their information differently, using different forms of language, if they make different assessments of the degree of knowledge which their interlocutor shares with them. In most everyday conversations which we record as examples of 'ecologically valid' conversations, the discourse analyst listens in on fragments of discourse broken out of other people's lives. It is not always possible for him to have access to the whole of the interaction, and he does not always know whether this is the first occasion on which the interactants have talked to each other, even whether it is the first occasion on which they have talked on this particular topic. He may not have, then, a basis for making claims about why one participant appears to treat a particular piece of information as 'shared' and another as 'news' to his interlocutor, EXCEPT in so far as the use of a particular FORM of expression may lead the analyst, as a member of the speech community, to assign a particular interpretation to the expression, on the basis of his previous experience of the function of that form, in a particular meaning structure, in a particular genre of discourse.

For many purposes, the more or less intuitive appeal to 'past similar experience of the use of a particular form' may yield a perfectly satisfactory basis for an analysis—particularly when the analysis is intended for other native speakers of the language who, the analyst may confidently expect, will share his speech-community-member's knowledge of the function of the relevant form, in a particular structure, in a particular genre of discourse. However, as soon as we enter the arena of foreign language teaching, the situation is changed. The hearer/reader may no longer have access to those intuitive interpretations which are available to members of the speech community of the discourse under analysis. It now becomes an obligation for the analyst to explain WHY he interprets such and such a form, in such and such a structure, in such and such a way.

Consider, for example, the use of indefinite expressions in discourse. How is the foreign hearer/reader to determine how to interpret an indefinite expression in a particular structure in a discourse? There seem to be a wide variety of answers available, which make claims which extend over indefinite expressions in any structure within a discourse:

(a) indefinite expressions mark THE FIRST MENTION of a referent (cf. e.g. Clark and Clark 1977);
(b) indefinite expressions mark the introduction into the discourse of brand-new referents WHICH ARE NOT IN ANY WAY KNOWN TO THE HEARER (cf. e.g. Prince 1981);
(c) indefinite expressions mark the introduction into the discourse of a referent which is an unidentified member of a set of referents WHICH MUST NUMBER MORE THAN ONE (cf. e.g. Hawkins 1978)

In spite of the fact that the claims made are general across discourse, it seems to be the case, if we examine naturally occurring discourse, that we can find examples of indefinite expressions being used in ways which do not seem to be helpfully characterized in any of these accounts. Consider the following extract from a conversation between a young Scotswoman K and her elderly cousin I, whom she has not met for several years:

I   where I stayed was in Mea+ was off Morningside Road
K   oh +yes+ that's not far from Granpa's house
K   yes + just further on + in the bus + you know THE PLAZA + there was A PLAZA + do you remember IT + further on
K   erm
I   it was the next stop

To many native speakers of English it will probably seem fairly clear what is happening here, and how the various forms of expression relating to 'the Plaza'—THE PLAZA—A PLAZA—IT—are being used by the speaker. To the foreign hearer/reader it may be less clear. Are the descriptive approaches to the indefinite expression which we have cited helpful to him? We note that the first mention actually takes the form of a definite expression, and the speaker appears to assume that the hearer will know 'the Plaza'—*you know the Plaza*. Even with respect to the expression *there was a Plaza*, it is not clear that 'the Plaza' the speaker is speaking of is 'unidentified', or expected to be unidentified by the hearer. What is intuitively clear to the native speaker may be quite difficult for him to express in a helpful, generalizable way: it does seem that there is a sense in which the speaker has 'changed her mind'. But what has she changed her mind with respect to? Why does she use an indefinite expression after having used a definite expression first? Is it because she realizes she has failed to follow a discourse rule about 'first mention'? Few native speakers will think that gives an adequate answer. Is it because she suddenly realizes that 'the Plaza' cannot in any way be known to the hearer? That seems too strong in the light of her next remark *do you remember it*. Is it because she thinks there is a set of 'Plazas' which the hearer may know about, but that she is unlikely to know about this particular one? That still seems somewhat off the mark. All of these accounts seem to relate to what we know about the use and distribution of indefinite expressions in discourse, but none of them gives a wholly satisfactory account of what seems to be going on here, in this particular discourse.

Is there a further set of generalizations which we could make, which might give us a better way of expressing what is going on here? How might we come by such generalizations?

9.1 THE METHODOLOGY OF ELICITING DATA

One way we can approach the problem is by eliciting controlled data, specially designed to provoke the kind of language we are interested in. The value of such data for the discourse analyst who wishes to give an account of the function and distribution of forms in particular genres of discourse is manifold:

(a) the analyst can control the nature of the task so that he can elicit comparable data from many different speakers and compare their output;
(b) he can control the relevant input to the task, so that he can perceive the specific information which a particular speaker has at the point when he produces a particular expression;
(c) he can be sure that the information relevant to the task in hand is new to all the participants at the beginning of an interaction—that it is not a fragment of some ongoing discussion between them;
(d) the language that is produced spontaneously by the participants.

Within the limitations of the controlled data, the analyst can examine regularities of language use and attempt to relate those regularities to a model which reflects the relevant aspects of states of speaker–hearer and of discourse construction. In the case of expressions used to refer, a constellation of such aspects needs to be considered. For the purposes of this chapter, the discussion is limited to the use and distribution of indefinite expressions. I believe that at least a partial account of this phenomenon can be given, in this limited genre of discourse, in terms of their knowledge, beliefs and intentions of speakers with respect to their hearers.

9.2 THE ELICITED DATA

The data under discussion are produced by Scottish 16-year-olds working in pairs. Speaker A is provided with the map of an island containing a set of dangerous natural features, which has a route marked across it to avoid the dangers. He is told that this is the most recent, hence most authoritative, map of the island. He is asked to describe the route to Speaker B. Speaker B has a map of the same island, a map which he is told represents the work of an early explorer, which is no longer entirely accurate. He is asked to draw on his map the route described by Speaker A. Speaker B's map contains most of the features on Speaker A's map, but not all. In addition, Speaker B has two features which are not shown on Speaker A's map. There are several noteworthy features about this task-design:

(i) No single speaker commands all the relevant knowledge. Speaker A is put in the authoritative position. Nonetheless he will have to take account of Speaker B's, sometimes incompatible, information.
(ii) Whereas for Speaker A the route is known, which contains his focus of attention to the next move in the map, for Speaker B the route is unknown, so he may scan and mention much larger areas of the map than Speaker A wishes to take account of. Speaker A may ignore or dismiss as unhelpful some of Speaker B's contributions. There is, then, a built-in feature of uncertainty or riskiness.
(iii) The task puts a considerable cognitive burden on both participants, particularly Speaker A. Speaker A has not only to plan and execute a set of route instructions, but also to accommodate another view of the current state of affairs as provided by B.
(iv) Participants give every sign of enjoying the task.

I shall concentrate here on two areas in the map where the participants have discrepant information:

(i) Both speakers have a palm beach in the bottom RH corner of the map and a huge waterfall in the bottom LH corner. A has a swamp lying between these features. B has no swamp but does have crocodiles there.
(ii) Both speakers have a Big River marked on the map, but only A has a bridge across this river.

Here are some typical extracts of interchanges at these two points.

SWAMP/CROCODILES

(1) C&D   A: have you got WEE PALM TREES aye?   B: ʌhʌ
have you got A WATERFALL?   aye
go + between THE PALM TREES and
THE WATERFALL

                                           but I've got
                                           CROCODILES
you've got what?   CROCODILES
whereabout?   in between
                                             THE WATERFALL
                                             and THE PALM
                                             TREES
right + go between THE
CROCODILES and THE PALM TREES

(2) E&J   A: go along and see where it says
'SWAMP'   B: no + I've not got
                                             ONE
go round about + and then come
round   I've not got A
                                             SWAMP
                                             I've got a
                                             PALM BEACH
see where THE PALM BEACH IS
then + make a C + that's going
round THE SWAMP

BIG RIVER/BRIDGE

(3) G&O   A: have you got a RIVER?   B: no
you've not + have you got
A BRIDGE?   no + got A BIG
                                             RIVER
aye + THAT'll do + go up
towards the river + just near
THE BRIDGE   I've not got A
                                             BRIDGE

9.3 SPEAKERS' MODELS OF HEARERS' KNOWLEDGE

Each speaker has two sources of knowledge which relate specifically to this task:

(i) what he can see on his own map;
(ii) what the other speaker claims to have, or not to have, on his map

Each speaker is in doubt about aspects of his hearer's map which he has not been told about. There appear to be a limited number of states of knowledge[2] which a speaker may have with respect to what he knows (from his map and what the other speaker has said) and what he does not know;

Sp H
	Sp	H	
(i)	+	+	speaker believes he and hearer both have this knowledge
(ii)	+	?	speaker knows he has and wonders if H has
(iii)	+	−	speaker knows he has but has learnt that H has not
(iv)	−	+	speaker has learned that he has not and that H has
(v)	?	?	speaker thinks he may have a relevant memory and wonders if H can pin it down. Consider 'wasn't there an old man who used to live there?' There are no examples of this sort in these data.

If we now look back at extracts from the cited data we can characterize the state of knowledge of the current speaker at the moment before he produces an utterance and note the form of expression which he provides. Consider first Speaker A, the authoritative current speaker, in extract (1):

	Current speaker	Current hearer	form produced
(1) A: have you got wee palm trees aye?	+	?	indef. plural
B: ʌhʌ̄			
A: have you got a waterfall?	+	?	A + noun
B: aye			
A: ... the palm trees and the waterfall	+/+	+/+	THE + noun, THE + noun
B: but I've got crocodiles			
A: ... what?			
B: crocodiles			
A: ... the crocodiles ... the palm trees	+	+	THE + noun

Consider the relevant chunk for Speaker B:

	Current speaker	Current hearer	form produced
B: but I've got crocodiles	+	?	indef. plural

Now consider Speaker B's state of knowledge in extract (2):

	Current speaker	Current hearer	form produced
(2) A: ... see where it says 'swamp'			
B: I've not got one	−	+	ONE
A: (presupposes B has)			
B: I've not got a swamp	−	+	A + noun
I've got a palm beach	+	?	A + noun

Consider the speakers in extract (3):

	Current speaker	Current hearer		Current hearer	Current speaker
A: . . . a river?	+	?	B. no	+	−
. . . you've not	+	−			
. . . a bridge?	+	?	no	+	−
			a Big river	?	+
that'll do	+	+			
. . . the river	+	+			
. . . the bridge	+	0	I've not got a bridge	+	−

The generalizations which appear to emerge from the data briefly represented here (we now have data produced by more than twenty pairs of students) are as follows:

(i) Where the current speaker believes his hearer's knowledge matches, (++), he uses a definite expression.
(ii) Where the current speaker believes his hearer doesn't share his information, (+−), he uses an indefinite expression.
(iii) Where the current speaker wonders whether his hearer shares his information, (+?), he uses an indefinite expression. Note that the speaker does not have to BELIEVE that his hearer lacks the relevant information; —he simply has to be in doubt.
(iv) Where the current speaker knows his hearer has information which he does not share, (−−), he may DENY presupposed knowledge using an indefinite expression, as in *I've not got a bridge*, or accommodate himself to his hearer's view using a definite expression, as in extract (1), last line, A's utterance *the crocodiles*.

That is to say, the speaker will tend TO USE AN INDEFINITE EXPRESSION WHEN HE WONDERS IF KNOWLEDGE IS NOT MUTUALLY SHARED. What he DOES with his utterance—ask a question, deny a presupposition etc.—will indicate which participant he assumes does have, or might have, the relevant knowledge.

Of course, the speaker will sometimes get it wrong: in the last line of extract (3), it appears that Speaker A assumes that Speaker B, having after all found 'a river', will also have found 'a bridge'—B denies this.

If we, necessarily tentatively, try to extrapolate the generalizations from these limited data to the conversation about 'the Plaza' where the speaker produced: *you know the Plaza* + *there was a Plaza? do you remember it?*, we appear to have at least a partially satisfactory account for the speaker's switch of forms. It appears that, initially, she assumes shared knowledge—*you know the Plaza*—then wonders if she is safe in doing so, and whether her interlocutor does have the knowledge (does remember) and produces *there was a Plaza*.

In the data that I have discussed, as in this last instance, the suggestion that the indefinite form is used not only when the speaker BELIEVES, but also if he SUSPECTS, that there may be a mismatch of knowledge, does seem plausible. It may not offer a total account of the value we assign to indefinite expressions in interpreting them in particular contexts. But in these cases, at least, the notion of mismatch of knowledge seems to offer more insights than approaches like 'indefinites are used to mark first mention', 'indefinites introduce into the discourse referents which are not in any way known to the hearer', or than the view that indefinite expressions 'introduce into the discourse a referent which is an unidentified member of a set of referents which must number more than one'. Ordinary speakers do not operate with such hard-and-fast rules but operate, rather, with sensitive, moment-by-moment evaluation of their hearer's current state of knowledge. As in all other aspects of communication, such evaluation always involves risk.

NOTES

1. The data cited here come from an SED-funded Project, 'Listening comprehension'. I am grateful to Anne Anderson, Richard Shillcock and, particularly, to Nigel Shadbolt for imaginative discussion. A further report is to appear in the *Journal of Linguistics*.
2. An adequate account of the data would need to make appeal to a third level of analysis—what the speaker believes the hearer believes about his (the speaker's) current state of knowledge. The notion of presupposition can only be captured by a model which includes this depth of processing. This chapter is a necessarily abbreviated and simplified attempt to show that this type of approach may yield insights into the distribution and function of particular forms (cf. Brown and Shadbolt forthcoming for extended discussion).

Part III
Comparative discourse studies

The four chapters in this final section—Hatim on discourse context and text-type, Hartmann on contrastive textology and bilingual lexicography, Krenn on 'extended reference', and Haden on discourse error analysis—illustrate some of the applications of modern textual analysis in areas such as language teaching, lexicography and translation. They also show how a contrastive perspective over more than one language can shed light on matters of general theoretical importance. So this is not merely an 'applications' chapter. The same theoretical principles that pervade this book—of meaning as function in context, and of theoretical work being enriched by the close study of specific aspects of natural language—are equally relevant in the environment of cross-language studies. Nevertheless, it is particularly important in a volume of this nature to go beyond the boundaries of English and to look at both universal and language-specific aspects of textual studies.

Hatim draws on problems associated with translating between Arabic and English to demonstrate again the importance of context, even in written texts. Specifically, he shows the importance of the interaction between the reader and the text. Even more than in speech, the decoder sets up hypotheses about the text type on the basis of signals in the lexicogrammar. Hatim sees context as an abstract set of instructions leading to hypotheses which are confirmed or not as the processing of the text advances. He demonstrates how mis-apprehension of the text-typological focus of a text can seriously disrupt otherwise competent translations. Not only is the field of the text 'about', say, OPEC, but the fact that the author is setting up a thesis to be supported or denied must also be appreciated and conveyed in the translation.

In addition to the interaction between the author and the reader, there can also be mediated interactional meanings in the events reported. Thus it can be crucial to make clear whether the refusal of a piece of information is presented politely or in the form of a rebuke by the interviewee, and judgement on these matters of interactional meaning shades off into areas beyond 'pure' linguistics.

Hatim, like Arndt in Part I, proposes a group of text-types—EXPOSITION, ARGUMENTATION and INSTRUCTION—which he sees language users referring to in hypothesis-using and testing. His discussion combines British Systemic work with European TEXTLINGUISTIK. He describes the context for a written text as primarily a rhetorical function, which is a central determiner in the construction of the text. The text producer sets up a series of macro- and micro-expectations at clause level and above, and must then fulfil these exactly, with no additional material and no loose ends. Texture is the realization of these expectations in language. In a close analysis of a text translated first into Arabic using nominal sentence types, and then verbal sentence types, he demonstrates how these two types signal different rhetorical functions. This exercise in contrastive textology supports the psychological reality of the notion of text-type in natural language use. In this he shows interesting parallels with Meyer's chapter in Part I.

Hartmann also takes contrastive textology as his theme, this time applying it to a text produced from the first in English and German versions by the authors, who are bilingual in both languages. He then examines in detail some verbal equivalences they have selected and compares them with a standard dictionary. By looking at the problems that face bilingual dictionary-makers, he draws attention to the role of parallel texts in dictionary production. Bilingual dictionaries, no less than monolingual ones, have to be based on real language in as many contexts of use as possible. Recourse to other dictionaries was never an adequate substitute,and it is now becoming less necessary with the technological developments at our disposal.

All kinds of dictionary have to distil generalizations about the behaviour of words from texts. By delivering collocational information they are also indicating constraints on how phrasal and sentential structures can be realized, under the additional handicap that just as semantic equivalence can be context-dependent, so also can lexical solidarity. The field, mode and tenor of a text can all influence the choice of items used. Furthermore, dictionaries themselves have to be seen as texts and as such can only be understood in the contexts of their use. They have an instructional function, which ideally ought to discriminate, for instance, between users who are interested primarily in comprehension and users who are producing translations. All of this points to more awareness of textology in lexicography, especially in contrastive lexicography.

Like Hatim, Krenn is interested in the segmentation of texts and the difficult decisions translators have to make. Specifically, she is interested in how the reference systems in English and German are exploited to structure texts. Brown, in her paper in Part II, looked at reference to specific entities in the experimentally created situation—what Krenn calls DISCRETE REFERENCE. Krenn, on the other hand, is concerned with EXTENDED REFERENCE. In this she includes not only pronominally signalled structures but also verbal expressions, such as *tell*, with and without nominals and, of course, what I have called 'unfulfilled lexical items'. This type of expression is used to create higher-order entities as a means of categorizing parts of the text message, sometimes in terms of the kinds of clause relations discussed by Meyer, sometimes in other more abstract ways, such as evaluation of indirect discourse. Particularly interesting in Krenn's contribution is the painstaking and exhaustive collection of tokens of this system in English and German.

Finally, we come to Haden's paper on discourse error analysis, where he looks at several ways in which contrastive textology can be applied to foreign language teaching. This study reflects the increased emphasis recently on the importance of communicative competence in foreign language work. No longer is it considered adequate only to give the foreign language learner structural competence in the syntax and familiarity with large amounts of vocabulary. Now it is hoped that the learner will also be enabled to take part in the kinds of interaction appropriate to the society where the language is spoken. This is at the same time both basic and very complex. As Hatim demonstrated, such a task is full of pitfalls. There are sources of interaction errors even in the most apparently straightforward activities. Well-known examples include the difference between Japanese and English negation, where the English *Yes* to a negative question like *Haven't you finished* contradicts the belief expressed by the sentence—*Yes. I have*; while in Japanese it would agree with it—*Yes. You are correct. I haven't finished*. Haden gives similar examples from French, Russian and Polish, related to reciprocity, hypothesizing, and vouching for the truth of a report. Here the problem is to appreciate the significance of the signals of the illocutionary act being performed. Other areas of difficulty derive from the problems of producing texture, whether in terms of the information structure or weighting, or of striking an appropriate interpersonal tone.

10 A text linguistic model for the analysis of discourse errors: contributions from Arabic linguistics*

Basil Hatim
University of Salford

The aim of this paper is to identify a number of problems in the use of language and to argue that these and similar problems can only be adequately accounted for within a model of discourse processing which takes a comprehensive view of context and relates it to text structure and texture. The various components of this heuristic model will be presented and each will be illustrated by an authentic example of a communication breakdown from translating, interpreting or general language use.

While the various examples are for practical reasons presented in English, the original source or target language was in most cases Arabic. Reference will therefore be made to how Arabic handles certain strands of textuality, particularly in the way it utilizes texture to reflect the context and structure of text. It is hoped that such linguistic features, which have received minimal attention from Arabic grammarians, will clearly demonstrate the psycho-logical reality of the model claimed here to account for discourse processing in general and explicate discourse errors in particular.

10.1 DISCOURSE/TEXT CONTEXT

The DISCOURSE/TEXT[1] processing model to be outlined here rests on the basic assumption that language users, producers and receivers alike approach discourse/text firstly by reacting to and interacting with the various strands of CONTEXT. This is attempted through a process of reconstruction which identifies a number of variables within three contextual domains of activity:

(a) PRAGMATIC ACTION on the environment. This refers to what discourse producers attempt to achieve, and discourse receivers pursue and accept, as the purpose of communication (e.g. 'to produce a rebuttal').
(b) SEMIOTIC INTERACTION with the environment. Here discourse/texts take on values which define them as signs in some symbolic system (e.g. 'a rebuttal preceded by a certain title and followed by a review of current trends').

* My thanks are due to participants in the series of seminars on text linguistics at Salford University for helpful comments and criticisms.

(c) COMMUNICATIVE TRANSACTION in the environment. This sets a framework
in which communication takes place by defining aspects such as time–
place, addressor–addressee, field of discourse, text mode etc. (e.g. an
editorial in a prestigious British daily).[2]

Consider the following language sample which illustrates the above
contextual categories:

Text A
 The Cohesion of OPEC
 Tomorrow's meeting of OPEC is a different affair. Certainly, it is formally
 about prices and about Saudi Arabia's determination to keep them down.
 Certainly, it will also have immediate implications for the price of petrol,
 especially for Britain which recently lowered its price of North Sea Oil and
 may now have to raise it again. But this meeting, called at short notice, and
 confirmed only after the most intensive round of preliminary discussions
 between the parties concerned, is not primarily about selling arrangements
 between producer and consumer. It is primarily about the future cohesion
 of the organization itself.

This process of context reconstruction initially takes the form of a MACRO-
ANALYSIS which tentatively identifies pragmatic purposes, the ways they are
made accessible through semiotics, and finally how they are made communicatively operational. The examples given in (a), (b) and (c) for Text A
above are typical insights normally yielded by this type of analysis. They are
hypotheses to be confirmed or refuted, modified or jettisoned once text
unfolds and the testing process begins in the form of MICRO-ANALYSIS. This
sequentially monitors textual progression, constantly informed by initial
impressions.
    To illustrate micro-analysis, we begin with the title of Text A, 'The
Cohesion of OPEC'. In terms of certain rules and conventions which regulate
our knowledge of how the world works, the element in question opens up the
option system: 'initiate a rebuttal' *vis-à-vis* 'expound on OPEC'S cohesion' as
values related to pragmatic action. This is informed, enhanced and simul-
taneously made accessible when it acquires a semiotic value which defines it
as a sign ('a cohesive OPEC'), catalogues it in terms of similar signs (e.g. 'a
cohesive Politbureau') and in terms of dissimilar signs (e.g. 'NATO in
disarray'), and finally identifies it more as a case of the latter option. This is a
confirmation of a pragmatic option which now reads: 'initiate a rebuttal of
those who claim that tomorrow's meeting of OPEC is as usual about prices'.
A number of questions might cross one's mind at this stage. Why couldn't this
title signal 'a case for the cohesion of OPEC? Why couldn't this title initiate an
unbiased 'review of current trends'? The answer to these and similar
questions is provided by categories from the communicative transaction
which is taking place: the source is *The Times* and not an OPEC-controlled
propaganda sheet; it is an editorial and not a survey article. At the same time

as pragmasemiotics is being negotiated, communicative insights such as these are brought to bear in the analysis of the ultimate effect.

Text B1 and B2 below illustrate how a mishandling of the contextual categories outlined above can lead to serious problems in communicating a message. In B1 (an authentic text) the Tunisian minister answers the question in Arabic in more or less the same form in which it appears here in English. A liaison interpreter conveys the answer to the American journalist in English. As Text B2 (a model translation) clearly shows, the minister pragmatically intends to perform the act of 'rebuking' his interviewer and semiotically aims at producing a 'thwarted exchange' which is also communicatively 'strained'. The rendering in Text B1, however, does not capture any of these features. What we have instead is a much more 'positive' response pragmatically, which contributes to the smooth 'ongoingness' of the exchange semiotically and establishes 'cooperativeness' communicatively.

Text B1	Journalist:	What were the contents of the letter you handed to King Fahad?
	Minister:	The question of the letter concerns the Saudis.
Text B2	Journalist:	....
	Minister:	I feel that is solely a matter for the Saudis to consider.

The result of this, as can be anticipated, is that the interviewer has felt invited to pursue this line of questioning.

10.2 TEXT-TYPOLOGICAL FOCUS

At the stage when micro-analysis gets under way and the testing of hypotheses yielded by macro-analysis begins, a basic hypothesis is developed. This relates to the predominance of a specific TEXT-TYPOLOGICAL FOCUS as a result of conflating pragmatic action and semiotic interaction within a communicative transaction. It is a definition of discourse/text function which determines, to use terms from de Beaugrande and Dressler (1981: 186), the efficiency, effectiveness and appropriateness of textual occurrences. For example, the macro-micro-analysis of the title and, say, the first two clauses in Text A above must take on values related to text-type for the analysis to be complete ('a counter-argumentative text unfolding'). Without such specification, language users would still be operating with a concatenation of sentences and not a cohesive and coherent text.[3]

Taking into consideration the highly variable and volatile nature of the text function constellations which accounts for the fuzziness characteristic of hybrid discourse forms, the following is a tentative list of basic text-types to which language users refer in producing and predicting discoursal occurrences:

1. EXPOSITION. This can be descriptive, focusing on objects and relations in space; Narrative, focusing on events and relations in time; Conceptual, focusing on concepts and relations in terms of either analysis or synthesis.
2. ARGUMENTATION. This can be Overt Argumentation (as in the counter-argumentative letter to the editor) or Covert Argumentation (as in the case-making propaganda sheet). Both forms are 'conceptual expository + evaluative' to distinguish them from Conceptual Exposition proper which is, by definition, '−evaluative'.
3. INSTRUCTION. This aims at the formation of future behaviour, either in Instruction With Option (as in advertising) or Instruction With No Option (as in treaties, contracts and other binding legal documents).[4]

As an example to illustrate a breakdown in communication due to a misappreciation of text-typological focus, consider Text C, which is a reworking of Text A. Text C is a literal English translation of the on-sight Arabic rendering of Text A offered by nine out of twelve students in a translation class.

Text C
Tomorrow's OPEC meeting is a different affair, because it is certainly about prices and about Saudi Arabia's determination to keep them down, and it will certainly have implications for the price of petrol, especially for Britain which recently lowered its price of North Sea Oil and may now have to raise it again. This meeting . . .

Basically, the error here is confusing the concessive (*certainly it is*) with a causal relationship (*because it is certainly*). The oppositive '*But this meeting* . . .' is also omitted, thereby producing a non-evaluative analysis (i.e. exposition).

10.3 TEXT STRUCTURE

Having formed hypotheses related to what may be termed RHETORICAL FUNCTION (a pragmatic–semiotic–communicative construct) and the resultant text-typological focus, the text receiver now proceeds with the micro-analysis, constantly informing and being regulated by macro-analysis, by negotiating text structure. Structure refers collectively to the various principles and basic assumptions involved in sectionalizing discourse into its immediate realizates. A basic hypothesis at work here is that CONTEXT (PRIMARILY RHETORICAL FUNCTION) ALMOST CAUSALLY DETERMINES THE WAYS A TEXT IS PUT TOGETHER.

Discourse is hierarchically organized in the fashion of Chinese boxes. It is realized by one or more texts which are in turn realized by one or more Suprasentential Entities SE. These take as realizates one or more Elements E which may be defined as a linguistic unit (e.g. clause or phrase) capable of fulfilling a rhetorical function and displaying a pragmatic–semiotic–communicative interface, thus pushing communication forward at the innermost level of discourse structure.[5] The following is a representation of Text A (section 10.1) in terms of the four levels of discourse organization.

Text A

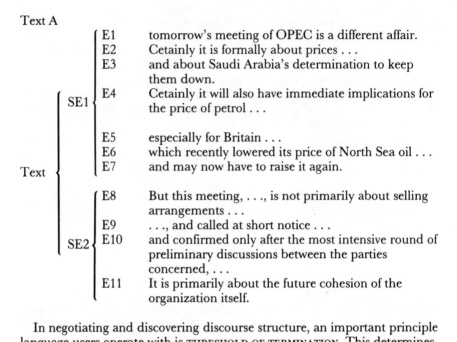

Text {
  SE1 {
E1   tomorrow's meeting of OPEC is a different affair.
E2   Cetainly it is formally about prices . . .
E3   and about Saudi Arabia's determination to keep them down.
E4   Cetainly it will also have immediate implications for the price of petrol . . .

E5   especially for Britain . . .
E6   which recently lowered its price of North Sea oil . . .
E7   and may now have to raise it again.

SE2 {
E8   But this meeting, . . ., is not primarily about selling arrangements . . .
E9   . . ., and called at short notice . . .
E10   and confirmed only after the most intensive round of preliminary discussions between the parties concerned, . . .
E11   It is primarily about the future cohesion of the organization itself.

In negotiating and discovering discourse structure, an important principle language users operate with is THRESHOLD OF TERMINATION. This determines, at any given level of discourse organization, the limit which renders the realize in question (E, SE, Text) INCOMPLETE, if not reached, or REDUNDANT if exceeded. In the words of de Beaugrande and Dressler (1981: 34): 'In principle, there is no cut-off point where production is definitely accomplished, but at most a THRESHOLD OF TERMINATION where the producer finds the outcome satisfactory for the intended purpose.'

To illustrate how a violation of the principle of Threshold of Termination can render texts redundant or incomplete and therefore deviant, consider Text D. It is taken from the work of an advanced learner of English as a foreign language. Material in parentheses has been edited out by native English proof-readers.

Text D

A third limitation (found in the present study) is related to the lack of (any serious) empirical backing for a number of notions introduced in the course of our discussion (and substantiated by our deliberations). For example, the model of text reception and production (developed) is highly intuitive. A psycholinguistic dimension (to be introduced into future research) might have filled the gap and shed some (useful) light on important aspects of text processing.

What has happened here is that at element level thresholds of termination are sometimes misperceived. For example, *the third limitation*, presupposes 'the two previous ones' which have already been identified as *found in the present study*.

Another basic principle at work in discourse structure negotiation is the COMMITMENT–RESPONSE pattern. This stipulates that at any level of discourse organization a commitment C is made by a given realizate to which a response R must be provided by a following realizate on the same level of discourse organization. This pattern is interrupted (i.e. no C is made and no R is expected) when a threshold of termination is reached.

Text A above provides an illustration of the C–R pattern at work in developing SE1. The following steps describe this process:

E1 'sets the scene' and makes a C to 'tackling the various aspects of the problem mentioned in E1 succinctly and comprehensively', the target for the SE to be developed being 'citation of a thesis to be opposed'.
E2 responds by dealing with 'aspect 1: prices' and makes a similar C to that made in E1.
E3 responds, highlighting certain features within aspect 1: 'Saudi role'.
E3 makes a similar C to that made in E1 and E2 and elicits an R in E4: tackling 'aspect 2: immediate implications'.
E5 highlights certain features within aspect 2: 'lowering oil prices' as an R to a C made in E4.
E6 in an R to a C made in E5 brings in 'the North Sea oil dimension' and makes a C to which an R is finally elicited in E7 related to 'what could happen as far as Britain is concerned'.
E1–E7 cover the basic aspects of the scene set, a threshold of termination is reached and a disjunction point in the C–R pattern is perceived.
E7 does not make a C to which an E8 may respond without lapsing into redundancy.
E1–E8 are packaged and the discourse is upgraded to a higher level of organization with SE1 emerging as 'thesis cited to be opposed'.

With negotiating and discovering SE1 as a starting point, the processing operation moves on to developing other SEs until a text emerges. SE1 makes a C to which an SE2 must respond with a 'statement of opposition' (*But this meeting . . .*). The process of structure negotiation is resumed on the Element level in an attempt to retrieve an SE with the required R in the following manner:

E8, E9, E10 and E11 together give rise to a 'counter-thesis'. A threshold of termination and a disjunction in the C–R pattern are perceived at E11–E12. E8–E11 are packaged and the discourse so far is declared to have attained the targets 'thesis cited and opposed'.
SE2 makes a C to which an R is to be found in SE3 'explication'.

Once this is achieved, SE3 will make a C to which an R is to be provided by SE4 'conclusion'. If this is managed successfully, no C will be made in SE4 to which an R is to be expected in SE5. A threshold of termination and a disjunction will be perceived, the four SEs packaged and the discourse so far declared to be a successful realisation of the rhetorical purpose 'overt argumentation' with Text 1 emerging as a token of the type in question.

An example to show how a misplaced threshold of termination and a misperceived disjunction in the commitment–response pattern can lead to incompleteness/redundancy is Text E1 below. The sample is taken from the kind of English typical of the English-medium press in, for example, the Arab World.

Text E1
   Babylon Company for TV Films
   The newly formed Babylon Company for the Production of Cinema and TV films decided to produce three TV serials in the coming months including 'The Lost Days' and an 'Evening Party'.
   It is noteworthy that Babylon Company was formed on February 7, 1980 with a capital of over ID6 million,

To identify the deviancy of the above text, we begin by analysing both the commitment–response pattern and the thresholds of termination underlying the discourse structure. Element 1 (*The newly formed*) makes a commitment ('designation to be attached') to which E2 (*Babylon Company for the Production of Cinema and TV Films*) provides a response ('object designated') and at the same time makes a commitment ('action to be attached'). E3 (*decided to produce three TV serials in the coming months*) provides an appropriate response ('action attached') and makes a commitment ('objects to be listed') to which E4 (*including. . .*) provides a response. E4 does not make a commitment as the highlighting function it serves is a typical threshold of termination. E1–E4 are packaged and Suprasentential Entity 1 emerges.

In text production/reception in general the initial SE makes a commitment, if only to be responded to by a zero-entity and thus cancelled. SE1 here makes a commitment to which any of the following options may be taken up as an appropriate response:

1. an explanatory note on one or all of the films cited;
2. another aspect of the company's activities;
3. etc.

In terms of communicative motivation, options 1 and 2 are ruled out as the function of the news report is to underline one basic function of the company (to produce three TV serials) and is not a film review. Whatever the third option is, it can never be a 'background note' as it is in the case in Text E1 above. This communicative function is, as should be, taken care of by E1. If the only new bit of information (the capital) is vital, it can by all means be added to that particular element. SE2 as it stands is redundant. The entity text should have emerged as soon as SE1 is completed, as the model Text E2 clearly shows.

Text E2   E1   The Babylon Company for the Production of Cinema and TV films

           E2   formed on February 7, 1980

     SE1 E3   with a capital of over ID6 million

           E4   has decided to produce three TV serials in the coming months

           E5   including 'The Lost Days' and an 'Evening Party'

     SE2   Ø

10.4 TEXTURE

A corollary to the basic context–structure hypothesis substantiated in section 10.3 above is the assumption that context (primarily rhetorical function), through such means as threshold of termination and commitment response (structure), almost causally determines the way discourse hangs together (texture). This includes devices such as cohesion, theme–rheme progression and kinds of information, collectively used in charting routes for the discovery of structure and context.[6]

In Text A (as displayed on page 106), the following texture devices (Table 10.1) are at work to facilitate structure negotiation and context reconstruction for SE1. E stands for Elements, CPA for Cohesive Pronominal Anaphora, FSP for Functional Sentence Perspective, with T–T indicating Theme to Theme Progression and R–T Rheme to Theme Progression, E1 for Evaluative Information and the symbol Ø for Ellipsis.

Table 10.1

E	CPA	FSP	E1
1	(meeting)	(meeting)	different
2	it	T–T	certainly. formally
3	it Ø	T–T Ø	certainly/formally Ø
4	it	T–T	certainly
5	it Ø	T–T Ø	certainly Ø

The cohesive effect cumulatively produced by the variables in Table 10.1 exhibits a systematic tailing-off which prepares for a threshold of termination to be reached and disjunction in the C–R pattern to be perceived at E7–E8. CPA shows the alternate loss and retrieval of the pronoun in E3, E5 and E2, E4 respectively. It also shows the complete loss of Pronominal Anaphora and a shift to Relativization which signals a highlighter normally associated with end-segments. This shift in E6 and E7 is also marked within FSP where the least turbulent T–T progression changes to an R–T progression normally associated with argumentation. A similar trend to that shown by CPA and FSP can be detected in the distribution of E1. This tailing-off effect is motivated in the sense that the text-typological instruction here is to 'cite a thesis compactly and comprehensively' and that, while E1–E5 tackle major aspects of the problem in question, E6 and E7 are there merely to enhance comprehensiveness in the treatment of the 'British situation' for the benefit of a predominantly British audience.

The problem of the deviation identified in Text C (p. 105) as one of misperceiving text-typological focus can also be explained in terms of disturbed texture flow which led to the production of conceptual exposition instead of overt counter-argumentation. The use of *because* and the change in the occurrence order of *certainly* which entailed the omission of *but* are some of the responses made by the receiver–interpreter who, having misperceived the intended text-typological focus, is nevertheless operating within the bounds of a sound, but mistaken, hypothesis (i.e. producing conceptual exposition).

10.5 CONTRASTIVE TEXTOLOGY

Having demonstrated the viability of our model of text processing outlined in the preceding sections in accounting for serious deviations in the use of language, and having underlined the fact that such deviations transcend inability to handle variables such as field, mode and tenor which are basic to analytic frameworks such as that of REGISTER,[7] my aim in this section is to pursue the ways context controls the unfolding of text-hierarchic structure and the deployment of various texture devices in Arabic. The object of the exercise is twofold: to provide evidence from a language other than English in support of our basic assumption underlying our initial hypothesis, namely that the notion of text-type is a psycholinguistic reality among speakers of natural language; and to inject our analysis with a contrastive dimension that should prove helpful in advocating the efficacy and workability of our model.[8]

Let us first consider some rudimentary facts of Arabic grammar. Using the sentence and its parts as basic units for analysis, Arabic grammarians identify two major clause types: the NOMINAL, which begins with the Subject (substantive or pronoun), for example, / ʔanta nabi:lun / 'you noble' *You are noble' and the* VERBAL, which begins with the verb and has the Subject as the Predicate, for example, / ma:ta muħamad / 'died mohammad' *Mohammad died*.

Operating within the constraints and limitations of the sentence, those grammarians with whose works I am acquainted had nothing of particular significance to say about the distinction between verbal and nominal sentence types in terms of their rhetorical/discoursal values. According to Wright (1859; revised 1955: 251–2): 'The difference between verbal and nominal sentences, to which the native grammarians attach no small importance, is properly this, that the former relates an act or event, the latter gives a description of a person or a thing . . .'

The discourse processing model outlined above, however, sheds new light on the discoursal values these two clause types take on as texture is mobilized

Table 10.2

Element	Clause type in original Arabic
1 Tomorrow's meeting of OPEC is . . .	N
2 Certainly it is . . .	N
3 and (it is) . . .	N
4 Certainly it will . . .	N
5 (it will) . . .	N
6 which recently lowered . . .	N
7 and may . . .	N
8 But this meeting, . . ., is . . .	N
9 , called . . .,	V
10 and confirmed . . .	V
11 It is . . .	N
. . .	(the rest is all verbal)

Table 10.3

Element	Clause type
1 Tomorrow's OPEC meeting is . . .	V
2 because it is . . .	V
3 and (it is) . . .	V
4 and it will . . .	V
5 (it will) . . .	V
6 which recently lowered . . .	V
7 and may . . .	V
8 This meeting is . . .	V
	(the rest is all verbal)

to manifest context and structure fluctuations. Consider in Table 10.2 the deployment of the verbal V and nominal N structures in an authoritative translation of Text A (as displayed on p. 103) into Arabic. Now in Table 10.3 consider the distribution of the two structures in an authoritative translation of Text C (p. 105).

The verbal structure in Arabic may best be looked at as the unmarked form used throughout in the absence of any contextual instructor pointing to a shift in text-typological focus, which, in the case of argumentation, necessitates the use of the nominal structure. Put differently, any shift from descriptive, narrative and conceptual exposition which utilizes the verbal form is construed as a shift in text-typological focus which requires a concomitant shift to structures other than verbal.

The representation of Text C in Table 10.3 is a demonstration of the hypothesis presented in the preceding paragraph and requires no further comment. Text A, represented in Table 10.2, however, may give rise to controversy. It could be argued that in the light of our hypothesis above, E1–E7, which 'cite a thesis' and therefore display an expository focus, should utilize the verbal clause structure. My basic counter-argument is that citing a thesis in order to OPPOSE it, a case illustrated by Text A, is different from citing a thesis in order to SUBSTANTIATE it. In overt argumentation (e.g. counter-argumentation), the transition between citing a thesis and opposing it is normally made smoother by underlining 'opposition' as the predominant focus and relegating the citation of 'the thesis opposed' to a secondary position. This is achieved in English, for example, by the use of certain semantic and syntactic texture devices aiming at producing what is known in rhetorical analysis as the STRAW MAN GAMBIT, that is, gaps which relay basic, in-built weaknesses in the thesis being cited. The use of *certainly* in Text A illustrates this notion from English. Arabic, on the other hand, achieves the transition more explicitly by the use of the nominal form which could be looked at here in terms of a CONTAMINATING EFFECT exercised by the main focus of the text.

This explanation might give rise to another possible criticism of our model's handling of overt argumentation, namely, that if opposition exercises a contaminating effect on the expository texture when the latter is of secondary focus, why do we not find the same effect being exercised on the rest of the text? Our answer to this is that it is only what precedes that is susceptible to contamination on the grounds that once the opposition is articulated, an expository force is needed to lend explications and conclusions credibility and to neutralize the contentious nature of the entire discourse. This highly intuitive explanation also accounts for why E9 and E10 are singled out and presented in the verbal form despite their position in the oppositive slot. They are part of the explication providing uncontentious background information and conceptually occurring in a post-oppositive slot.

10.6 SUGGESTIONS FOR FURTHER RESEARCH

The analysis of the above texts has underlined the need for further research into discourse complexity and made us aware of the danger of restricting oneself to the well-charted paths of basic formats. Working with more complex texts should yield rigorous criteria for identifying basic text-types and, far more importantly from the language teacher's viewpoint, basic forms which are tokens of such types. From this should follow comprehensive lists of basic text samples which illustrate the various text forms for use in a number of activities within applied linguistics. For example, from my own rudimentary research into the text-type 'argumentation', a very interesting 'counter-argumentative' form has emerged. This can be considered a token of the type 'case-making' as opposed to the more straightforward form 'counter-argumentation' illustrated by Text A above.

Text F

E2	In the following pages, the Arab Research Centre presents a constructive DISCUSSION on Nasser and his policies,
E2	held by TWO AUTHORS belonging to two DIFFERENT CULTURES.
E3	ONE IS BRITISH,
E4	WHILE the OTHER is an Arab.
E5	The British author is ....
E6	....
	....
E9	The Arab author is ....
	....
E10	....
	....

The emphasized words are vital clues to the fact that the text under analysis is expository + evaluative and that a case is being made and argued for. In Arabic, to signal this evaluative focus, the nominal clause type is used in presenting E3, E4, E5 and E9, being the Elements introducing the two basic sides of the evaluation. The second aspect of the evaluation (E9) is introduced by / ?amma / 'as to X', *On the other hand*, even when it is implicit in English.

NOTES

1. TEXT, as opposed to DISCOURSE, is the string of 'sentences' which map a set of communicative intentions on to the linguistic surface with the aim of fulfilling a particular rhetorical purpose.
2. For a comprehensive treatment of discourse PRAGMATICS, see van Dijk 1977. For an overview of discourse SEMIOTICS, see Nöth 1977. A useful summary of basic work on the COMMUNICATIVE aspects of discourse context can be found in Enkvist 1977.
3. For an excellent survey of the evolution of text-linguistics, as well as a lucid presentation of basic text-linguistic notions, see de Beaugrande and Dressler 1981.
4. On the notion of TEXT-TYPE from an applied-linguistic point of view, see Werlich 1976.
5. For pioneering work on discourse STRUCTURE, see Gleason 1968 and Hasan 1977.
6. On COHESION, see Halliday and Hasan 1976; on FSP, see Daneš 1974; on KINDS OF INFORMATION, see Grimes 1975; and for a more specialized treatment of TEXTURE, see de Beaugrande 1980.
7. For a theoretical argument against the notion of REGISTER as traditionally practised, see Hatim forthcoming. A critique of traditional REGISTER ANALYSIS from an applied-linguistic point of view, with an alternative presented as a contribution to curriculum design, see Hatim 1984.
8. On CONTRASTIVE TEXTOLOGY, see Hartmann 1980 and James 1983.

11 Contrastive textology and bilingual lexicography

R. R. K. Hartmann
University of Exeter

This chapter explores the relevance of discourse patterns to lexicography. Specifically, I want to examine some possibilities of contrasting vocabulary structure in a pair of languages like English and German by relating the notion of 'parallel texts' to the problem of interlingual equivalence in dictionary-making.

I do not apologize for introducing the contrastive or bilingual perspective into the programme; indeed, I believe it to be absolutely essential both in terms of text theory and applied linguistics. And in the field of lexicography, which is only just becoming aware of its history and position within and *vis-à-vis* the linguistic sciences, such a perspective can only bring benefits. One could even claim that bilingual lexicography is one of the oldest branches of applied linguistics!

Contrastive textology is basically the combination of two complementary approaches: comparative or contrastive analysis on the one hand, and textual or discourse analysis on the other. There is not time here to develop this theme at length, but what it boils down to is the view that any theory of language which neglects both the dimension of difference or diversity and the dimension of text or context is widely off the mark.

There is no need to offer a long line of authorities and models to back up the idea of a contrastive textology (cf. Hartmann 1980). I shall instead go straight to a specific example. The passages that I have reproduced below are what I call 'parallel texts'. They come from the introduction to text linguistics published in 1981 in simultaneous English and German versions by Robert de Beaugrande and Wolfgang Dressler.

(1) Parallel texts

A TEXT will be defined as a COMMUNICATION OCCURRENCE which meets seven standards of TEXTUALITY. If any of these standards is not considered to have been satisfied, the text will not be communicative. Hence, non-communicative texts are treated as non-texts (cf. III. 8). We shall outline the seven standards

Wir definieren einen TEXT als eine KOMMUNIKATIVE OKKURRENZ (engl. 'occurrence'), die sieben Kriterien der TEXTUALITÄT erfüllt. Wenn irgendeines dieser Kriterien als nicht erfüllt betrachtet wird, so gilt der Text nicht als kommunikative. Daher werden nicht-kommunikative Texte als Nicht-Texte behandelt (vgl.

informally in this chapter and then devote individual chapters to them later on.

III. 8). Hier werden wir diese sieben Kriterien informell skizzieren, später aber jedem von ihnen ein eigenes Kapitel widmen.

[Beaugrande and Dressler 1981, section 1.3]

I hope you agree that this is a happy choice: the extract allows us not only to illustrate their approach, but to use it to demonstrate how contrastive text analysis can benefit bilingual lexicography.

The definition that Beaugrande and Dressler give of TEXT and TEXTUALITY applies, of course, to the text sample in front of us. But, I suppose, for the definition to make sense, I ought at least to mention these famous seven standards that must be met to make this particular stretch of discourse a text rather than a non-text. I will briefly list them and say how they apply here:

1. COHESION
2. COHERENCE
3. INTENTIONALITY
4. ACCEPTABILITY
5. INFORMATIVITY
6. SITUATIONALITY
7. INTERTEXTUALITY

Our two texts cetainly have COHESION: the successive elements hang together without a break, with the exception perhaps of the cross-reference to a section in a later chapter.

COHERENCE is the mutual relevance of the underlying knowledge of the world: you do not have to be a specialist in text linguistics to make sense of the passage.

INTENTIONALITY relates to the wish of the text producer (two in this case) to give the message a proper shape: it certainly has that.

And, from the text receiver's point of view, it is ACCEPTABLE within normal bounds of inference, unless you completely disagree with this kind of framework.

INFORMATIVITY or the relationship of a message to known or expected information is also given here, except that some of you may be puzzled by the circularity of the definition.

SITUATIONALITY is the relevance to a communicative context. It is certainly appropriate to find a definition in a paragraph which is part of a chapter headed 'Basic notions'.

Finally, INTERTEXTUALITY refers to the fact that most texts have to fit with the conventions of the genre of which they are part: ours is clearly in the familiar argumentative style of the textbook (no pun intended).

Why should this kind of discourse analysis or textology be of interest to the lexicographer? There are several reasons:

— because it can support the lexicographer's intuitive grasp of language in particular contexts: it can, for instance, provide evidence for the predominance or grammatical characteristics of certain vocabulary items in certain language varieties;

— because it can help select and document particular text-types or styles or registers or genres: it can, for example, provide samples to illustrate the ranges and differences between certain varieties;

— because it can bring out features of the language that have been neglected or ignored: it can, for example, highlight the frequency of a particular collocation in a certain text-type.

Dictionary-makers will of course say that they have always used textual evidence (many even give examples in the form of direct quotations), but in the majority of cases this evidence has been diluted or indirect: diluted when the lexicographer has relied on his own intuitions as a native speaker; indirect when he was wittingly or unconsciously 'borrowed' from other dictionaries. As a compiler of a terminological dictionary of the language of linguistics and reviewer of numerous dictionaries, I know how widespread these practices are, and there are plenty of references in the literature (e.g. Zgusta 1971) which suggest or even recommend that monolingual dictionaries should be used as a data base for bilingual ones!

I would claim that in bilingual lexicography it is particularly important that the decisions of the compilers should be supported by a corpus of parallel texts. I will just give one brief example from our parallel texts in (1) above, in particular the expression *meet* or *satisfy the standards* and its German counterpart *Kriterien erfüllen*. Now you will agree, I am sure, that these are fairly straightforward and not at all unusual phrases which one would expect to find in the average bilingual dictionary.

I checked in one which is both recent and considered by many to be one of the best, the *Collins German Dictionary*. If you look in the English–German part, you will indeed find the entry *standard*, together with one or two verb collocations like *set a standard* and *conform to a standard*, but not *meet* or *satisfy the standards*. You will find as German equivalents *Norm* and *Maßstab*, but not *Kriterium*, although in the German–English part *Maßstab* leads to *standard* (which is defined as *Kriterium*). If you look up the verbs *satisfy* and *meet*, you will find noun collocations with *conditions* and *demands* (but not *standards*) and the verb equivalent *erfüllen*, together with others. You do not fare much better if you consult the German–English part. If you look up *Kriterien*, or rather the singular *Kriterium*, you find neither the associated verb *erfüllen* nor the English equivalent *standard*.

Need I say more? Perhaps I will just say two things. First, it is quite clear that Terrel *et al.* 1980 had not come across our text, which is statistically highly improbable unless they are aficionados of text linguistics. Secondly, and hopefully, the technological marvels of word-processing and computing could help eliminate the worst of such wild-goose chases.

I could go on to describe some of the types of parallel texts that have been studied by scholars in various fields such as translation studies, comparative stylistics and contrastive rhetoric. These range from wedding announcements and obituaries to language of instruction, politics and a number of literary texts and their equivalents in other languages. But I think it is time to move on to my second topic, which is the notion of 'equivalence'.

What meaning discrimination by definition achieves in the monolingual dictionary is achieved by giving equivalents in the bilingual dictionary. As Ladislav Zgusta says in the famous *Manual of Lexicography* (1971: 294), 'the basic purpose of a bilingual dictionary is to coordinate with the lexical units of one language those lexical units of another language which are equivalent in their lexical meaning', and we have already had a brief glimpse of the difficulties involved in the coordination of some lexical equivalents.

The branch of linguistics that is responsible for the coordination of vocabulary across language barriers is sometimes called 'contrastive lexicology' (cf. Hartmann 1976).

But this covers a number of very diverse approaches, with very different methods, if indeed they deserve the label 'methods'. The pioneer in what he himself called the 'structural semantics' of German and English was the Swiss linguist Ernst Leisi 1953. I mention him here specifically not only for what he and his pupils have achieved in this field, but also because his work has not received the acknowledgement it deserves in the literature (e.g. Di Pietro does not refer to him in his book *Language Structures in Contrast*, 1971.)

To take our earlier example again, contrastive lexicology has the job of explaining what place the verbs *meet*, *satisfy* and *erfüllen* have in the lexical structure of English and German, and what similarities and divergences exist in the vocabulary systems of these and any pair of languages. This is done, usually, by establishing so-called 'sets' or 'domains' or 'fields' of words with similar semantic and often also grammatical behaviour and then distinguishing the various members of the field by means of componential or distinctive feature analysis. There is also some attempt to display the relationships between the members of lexical fields by means of matrices or by using other graphic notations, such as overlapping circles or family tree diagrams.

We would see that verbs like *meet*, *satisfy*, *achieve* etc. on the one hand, and *erfüllen*, *einhalten* etc. on the other do not match exactly across the language boundary, even in such a neutral, international and non-descript kind of academic discourse as an introductory textbook. (It is no accident that in the extract we looked at earlier the single German verb *erfüllen* is matched with the two English synonyms *meet* and *satisfy*, in the first and second sentences.

However, there are a few snags with the more idealized models that have been put forward in contrastive lexicology. I have criticized some of these studies (including my own) on three grounds:

(i) Such studies do not take into account the actual operations by which bilinguals achieve equivalence. Equivalence is not a static correspondence, but the result of a conscious matching or approximation process in an interlingual context.

(ii) Such studies are often arbitrary, limited and tentative, using the sort of restricted data base that I would regard as artificial and inadequate.

(iii) Far from being an effective check on lexicographical work, such studies
     are often based directly or indirectly on the information given in existing
     bilingual dictionaries, and thus many of their shortcomings.

This criticism does not invalidate research in contrastive lexicology, but it
demands a higher standard of scientific method; and this includes, I think, a
greater reliance than hitherto on parallel texts.

Now you are going to ask me, quite rightly, what ARE the methods of
equivalance-seeking in bilingual lexicography? If contrastive lexicology has
not delivered the goods so far, where does the compiler of the bilingual
dictionary find his coordinated lexical units?

This is a very difficult question indeed, and I do not pretend that I have a
satisfactory answer, at least not a simple one. Part of the problem lies in the
notion of 'equivalence' itself: you cannot go out into the field and find ready
equivalents lying around at your disposal, except perhaps if you were to
stumble on a perfect dictionary (which, we all know, is still quite some
distance away!). Equivalence is not a concrete, given entity, but a relative,
fluid and relational concept: a lexical correspondence between two words or
expressions in a pair of languages does not exist until it has been established
as a result of a bilingual act, as I have suggested earlier. (The authors of our
parallel texts had to do a lot of careful double-checking to produce an
acceptable translation.)

We can of course try, as Zgusta 1971 and others have done, to classify the
various types of equivalents, and that is certainly a useful exercise for anyone
entering the field of bilingual lexicography. It will not take the newcomer long
to realize that complete, full or absolute equivalents are not all that frequent.
Examples from our extract are the words *text/Text*, *textuality/Textualität* (and
other close cognates used as technical terms), pairs like *seven/sieben* and
perhaps *treat/behandeln*. But the majority of equivalents will be incomplete,
partial or skewed. (I have already drawn your attention to some of the
problems of the near-equivalents *standards/Kriterien* and their collating verbs
meet, *satisfy* and *erfüllen*.)

There is even an example of something approaching a 'lexical gap' in our
texts: the German counterpart of *occurrence*, *Okkurrenz*, which does not sound
at all natural (if you are charitable, you call it translationese; if not, you may
call it a monstrosity), but the authors could not find anything more suitable
than the direct borrowing. Nor can I.

Most equivalents are, I would claim, not even one-to-two or one-to-many,
but many-to-many, a fact which I have tried to illustrate in the example with
the equivalent sentences *the text will not be communicative* and *der Text gilt nicht
als kommunikativ*.

(2) Many-to-many equivalents
E1 t. will be not c,
E2 T. WILL NOT BE C.   G2 *T. wird nich k. sein
E3 t. is said to be not c.   G3 T. heißt nicht k.
E4 t. is not regarded as c.   G4 T. wird nicht als k. erachtet

E5 *t. is not valid as c. G5 T. GILT NICHT ALS K.

G6 T. gilt als nicht k.

We can represent these as deliberate choices from among a range of possibilities in each of the two languages, including the two versions E1 and G6 which are not only possible, but in this instance might perhaps even be preferable. We can also see that the more literal equivalents that a bilingual dictionary might have supplied would be definitely misleading the translator or language learner into producing a reading that would be clearly wrong or erroneous, for example, from E2 to *G2, or from G5 to *E5 (these are marked with the customary asterisk as 'unacceptable' or 'inappropriate' in this context).

But not only do we find that there are many different types of equivalents and that they are typically multiple. There are in my view at least five further complications that we must clear up if we are to get a truly satisfactory treatment of this problem in interlingual lexicography.

The first dimension of dictionary equivalence is MEANING DISCRIMINATION, a catch-all term which stands for a number of devices lexicographers use to separate the different senses of words and expressions, ranging from definitions and synonyms to illustrative contexts and usage labels. Thus, the various senses of both English *standard* and German *Kriterium* could be marked, showing that they are genuine equivalents only in one or two of these. This problem is particularly acute when the cultural differences between speech communities are wide.

The second dimension is DIRECTIONALITY OF TRANSFER. Several authorities have rightly pointed out that equivalence is not necessarily a symmetrical relation, and that convergences and divergences depend on the direction in which one switches between the languages (that is why terms like source and target language are used). Thus, if you consult the *Collins German–English Dictionary* under *devote* and *widmen*, you will find only partly overlapping sets of verb equivalents. Depending on what sorts of objects are given by whom to whom and for what purpose, you may be directed from *devote* to *widmen*, *verwenden* and *bestimmen* in one way, and from *widmen* to *dedicate*, *devote*, *attend to* and *apply oneself to* the other way (cf. Hausmann 1977).

The third dimension is PURPOSE OF TRANSFER. The information on equivalents may depend on whether the user needs to know what a given word in a text means or how he should express a particular idea, in other words, whether the purpose of the look-up is passive comprehension (as in reading) or active production (as in composition). It has been suggested that meaning discrimination should be sensitive to these different requirements (cf. Steiner 1977).

If you take this argument to its logical conclusion, you end up with at least four different types of bilingual dictionary: one to go from source language to target language, one to go from target language to source language, one for comprehension, and one for production. (In practice, dictionary publishers are reluctant, particularly for the rarer language combinations, to go to such lengths.)

The fourth dimension relates to the physical LOCATION of meaning discrimination devices inside the dictionary entry. There is some specialized literature developing (cf. Werner 1982) which on the basis of careful examination of lexicographical practices makes some interesting recommendations on where exactly usage labels should be put for maximum accuracy and consistency, for example, at the beginning of the entry if the headword is ALWAYS used in a particular way, or at a particular sub-entry which covers a certain sense of the word in the source language, or at the appropriate equivalent in the target language. In any case, labelling should only be used if the equivalents do not behave identically in the same context, for instance, if they do not come from corresponding speech styles.

The fifth and final dimension is one that I believe has so far not been considered in earnest, although it conditions many (if not all) of the other aspects of equivalence in the bilingual dictionary. This is the CODE-SWITCHING skill of bilingual speakers who bring about the sorts of equations and coordinations that lexicographers draw on. What I am suggesting is that for most language pairs a body of partly codified and partly untapped, but in any case highly volatile matching vocabulary is activated during acts of inter-lingual communication—typically in such areas as foreign language learning, translation and interpreting, but also in many other, more informal contact situations like international meetings. I can only hint at what is at present still rather unexplored, the sort of thing for which the parallel texts gave an illustration. Beaugrande and Dressler, as highly skilled, near-perfect bilingual linguists with much experience in translating, manage to hit the most appropriate equivalents in their textbook nearly every time. We can only hope and pray that the bilingual lexicographer takes as much care in his seeking, finding and presenting of lexical equivalents.

If and when he has done his job properly, he provides us as users of bilingual dictionaries with the means we need to cross the language barrier, either as decoders of texts (reading comprehension) or in encoding (text composition). And in this process the dictionary-maker becomes a text-producer: he creates a quite distinct genre of discourse, the dictionary as a succession of texts called 'entries'. The only linguist to have drawn attention to this phenomenon, as far as I know, is Herbert Ernst Wiegand. In a couple of exploratory papers (Wiegand forthcoming) he has characterized the typical dictionary entry as 'instructional discourse', akin to a textbook or technical manual, which issues directions to the potential dictionary-user on how a particular word or expression is used, that is, its spelling, semantic meaning, grammatical characteristics etc.

The following illustration is an attempt to describe the text type of the entry in a bilingual dictionary in such terms.

(3) Text structure of a dictionary entry

standard ['stændəd], *s.* **1.** *Mil:* Fahne *f;* **royal s.**, königliche Standarte *f.* **2.** *Meas:* Eichmaß *n; Ind:* Norm *f; Fin:* **the gold s.**, Goldwährung *f.* **3.** (*a*) (*yardstick*) Maßstab *m;* **to apply/set high standards**, hohe Maßstäbe anlegen/setzen; **to be up to s.**, den Anforderungen/*Ind:* der Norm entsprechen; **below s.**, ungenügend; (*of goods*) von minderwertiger Qualität; (*b*) (*level of achievement*) Niveau *n;* **to maintain standards,** das Niveau einhalten; **s. of living**, Lebensstandard *m;* **to aim at a high s.**, sich *dat* ein hohes Ziel setzen; ein hohes Niveau anstreben; (*c*) *pl.* (*values*) **moral standards**, moralische Werte; **to conform to normal standards of behaviour**, sich der Norm entsprechend verhalten. **4.** *attrib.* Standard-; (*a*) **s. work**, Standardwerk *n;* **s. English**, die englische Gemeinsprache; (*b*) *Ind:* (*of equipment etc.*) serienmäßig; **s. size**, Normalgröße *f;* **s. model**, Standardmodell *n;* serienmäßige Ausführung; *Aut:* **seat belts are s. equipment/are fitted as s.**, Gurte werden serienmäßig mitgeliefert; *Rail:* **s. gauge**, Normalspur *f.* **5. lamp s.**, Laternenpfahl *m; H:* **s. lamp**, Stehlampe *f; Hort:* **s. rose**, Hochstammrose *f.* **standardi′zation,** *s.* Standardisierung *f; Ind:* Normierung *f; Meas:* Eichung *f.* **′standardize,** *v.tr.* (etwas) standardisieren; *Ind:* (Produkte usw.) normieren; **to s. weights and measures**, Gewichte und Maße eichen.

[*Harrap's Concise Dictionary*, 1982: 390]

It is taken from the most recent German–English dictionary, the *Harrap's Concise* (Sawyers 1982), and covers some of the information that may be relevant to establish equivalence between the phrases *meet* or *satisfy standards* and *Kriterien erfüllen*, as discussed earlier. If it is true, as Wiegand claims, that lexicographical texts such as dictionary entries are designed to communicate something to the dictionary-user in order to help him solve a communication problem, then the text structure must be transparent to the person consulting the dictionary. The dictionary-user has to know where to find the information he seeks and how the elements he finds fit together in relation to the discourse at hand.

Every dictionary entry, like that on the lexeme *standard* in the *Harrap's Concise*, has textural cohesion and density, although it is usually composed of a number of diverse sub-entries and stands in a syntagmatic relationship to all the other entries. We can distinguish (with Hausmann 1977 and others) between the 'micro-structure' of the text within the entry and the 'macro-structure' of the text of the whole dictionary. We note that in this particular entry the distinction between micro- and macro-structure is somewhat blurred: for example, compounds like *gold standard*, *standard gauge* and *lamp standard* are scattered, apparently without rhyme or reason, over several sections of the entry, and related lexemes like *standardize* and *standardization*, which might have been (and are in other dictionaries) given separate headword status, are also contained within the micro-structure, thus possibly confusing the potential user. The internal arrangement of the five sub-entries of *standard* is presumably the result of conscious decisions on the part of the lexicographers, but the resulting textual structure may be in conflict with the average user's textual competence. Thus, faced with the problem of locating the appropriate German translation of the word *standard* in the phrase *meet* or *satisfy standards*, which of these five sub-entries or senses is the user to concentrate on, given that these collocations are not actually listed? By a process of elimination he might choose 3.(a) as the closest approximation, thus obtaining *Maßstab* (not *Kriterium*, which we know from our original parallel text, but a pretty close synonym). However (even if we limit ourselves to the internal evidence of *Harrap's* own macro-structure by doing some more cross-checking), this will not collocate very naturally with *erfüllen*, the verb that we may have unearthed, after a very long detour, as the best match for *meet* or *satisfy* in the sense of 'fulfil'. It would take considerable powers of paraphrasing on the part of the user to hit on *Kriterien erfüllen* from the information given in this dictionary. (Similar difficulties face the user in the other direction, by the way.)

It is easy to criticize dictionaries for their inconsistencies and their failure to include particular bits of information. It is much harder, but in my view more urgent, to improve communication between the dictionary-maker and the dictionary-user. One way in which I trust we can do this is by applying the findings of text linguistics and discourse analysis to lexicography. At the level of documentation, corpus-gathering and recording the notion of parallel texts can help refine the data base of the lexicographer; at the level of description, processing and editing contrastive lexicology, particularly when it is done in a textual context, can make the process of equivalence-seeking in bilingual lexicography more realistic; at the level of diffusion, presentation and publishing the textual approach—coupled with surveys of what dictionary-users actually need to do—can improve communication by making us aware of the conventions and strategies embodied in the textual structure of the dictionary and its entries.

12 'Extended reference' in English and German

Monika Krenn
University of Munich

12.1 INTRODUCTION

It seems difficult to find a single well-established term for the phenomena I should like to discuss in this chapter. The terms that come to mind are associated with narrower and also divergent definitions. What is more, the phenomena as such have rarely been accounted for in a systematic and comprehensive way. The term I have eventually settled on is that of 'extended reference'. It was originally introduced by Halliday and Hasan in *Cohesion in English* (1976: 52) and explained as reference to more than just a person or object, namely to a process or sequence of processes or, grammatically speaking, to a clause or string of clauses, not just a single nominal. As it stands, this definition could easily cover what they call 'text reference', 'verbal' and 'clausal substitution' and certain aspects of 'ellipsis' and 'lexical cohesion'. My aim here is in fact to bring together structures like these under the comprehensive label of 'extended reference'. I am as it were pleading for an extended 'extended reference'. I hope to show that evidence can be adduced for equivalence in terms of function of diverse lexical and grammatical items and constructions. Reference to non-discrete entities seems to be a mechanism essential to the functioning of discourse. It is, however, realized by different lexicogrammatical means in one and the same language as well as across languages. My aim in this chapter is to present a survey of the various forms 'extended reference' may take in English and in my mother tongue and to discuss selected examples. The texts I am quoting are modern short stories by German- and English-speaking authors in bilingual editions.

12.2 THE CONCEPT OF 'EXTENDED REFERENCE' AND THREE FUZZY DISTINCTIONS

12.2.1 'Extended' vs. 'discrete' reference

I propose that a distinction should be drawn between 'extended' and 'discrete' reference. The latter may be defined as reference to entities in the extralinguistic world, whether they are already mentioned in the text or not, which are established as such prior to the individual communicative event. By contrast, extended reference is the process of selecting a portion of information given situationally or activated by the foregoing discourse and of assigning it the status of a 'higher-order entity' (a term used by Lyons (1979: 93)). Extended reference has thus a creative and categorizing effect.

The distinction between extended and discrete reference is a fundamental one, although in practice it may be difficult to draw it. What follow are two instances of ambiguity which are particularly conspicuous when a translator has to opt for one or the other type of reference.

In the first example, with both a discrete entity and a larger stretch of discourse as possible antecedents, the English reference item *it* has two distinct readings. The ambiguity cannot be rendered in German. The translator decided on extended reference which is more likely in context.

(1) 'Miss Price, the invalid,' Mrs. Rowan said, 'insists on pouring the tea. She likes IT (IT gives her pleasure . . .)'

'Fräulein Price, die Invalidin', sagte Frau Rowan, 'besteht darauf, den Tee einzuschenken. Sie hat ES gern (ES bereitet ihr Vergnügen . . .)'

In the second example, the potential antecedents are not as clearly distinguishable, nor are the two interpretations of the reference item.

(2) She felt, however, that in such a crisis she must not give way to a private grief; and if she had a heart attack nobody heard of IT.

Sie fand aber, daß sie in so schwerer Lage ihrem persönlichen Kummer keinen Lauf lassen durfte, und wenn sie einen Herzanfall hatte, so erfuhr ES doch niemand.

The ambiguity of IT—ambiguity between 'heart attack' vs. 'having a heart attack'—might have been rendered in German by *davon hören*, but the translator chose not to or was not aware of the problem. The verb *erfahren* automatically selects the extended antecedent.

12.2.2 Exophoric vs. endophoric reference

It is no doubt important to draw a neat line between reference to the extralinguistic world and reference within discourse, a distinction for which Halliday and Hasan 1976 suggested the terms 'exophoric' vs. 'endophoric'. And yet there are numerous cases where it is impossible to determine whether we are dealing with one or the other. This is particularly true for extended reference because, quite obviously, it is easier to find out whether some state of affairs has been stated explicitly or evoked only indirectly. A problem specific to my corpus of texts is the duplication of the communication frame: the inner frame involves the protagonists of the narrative and what they communicate to each other, whether expressed in direct or reported speech;

the outer frame is constituted by the communication between author and reader. What is exophoric reference on the inner level may thus become endophoric reference in the narrative as a whole. To avoid these problems and because the distinction of endophoric vs. exophoric extended reference does not contribute a great deal to the main points of the argument here, I shall ignore it in what follows.

12.2.3 Referential vs. categorial identity

Extended reference in discourse, as I understand it here, is based either on referential identity or categorial identity (a question of principle which I must neglect here would be whether we can speak of referential identity of whole states of affairs in the way philosophers of language use the term 'reference'). To contrast these two subtypes seems to amount roughly to Halliday and Hasan's distinction between 'reference' and 'substitution' which I find problematic, however. A minor point might be that their 'comparative reference; is a hybrid concept anyway. What is more is that the two forms of identity can hardly be distinguished in many cases and this is particularly true for extended reference. At best, one can postulate two subtypes of basically the same mechanism in discourse. To show that it is not easy to draw a line between referential and categorial identity, and that reference items may be ambiguous in this respect, I should like to quote two examples where the translation changes referential identity into the weaker categorial identity.

(3) . . . einmal fragte er, ob er mir etwas erzählen könnte . . .
    Ich hatte schon längst darauf gewartet, daß DAS mal käme.

    . . . once he asked whether he might tell me something . . .
    I'd already long been expecting that SOMETHING OF THE KIND would emerge.

(4) (Context: a child is waiting for his father in front of a bar, but he has stolen away to get rid of the child.)

    THIS went on until half past two when snow began to fall.

    SO ging es weiter bis halb drei, als es anfing zu schneien.

12.3 STRUCTURAL DIVERSITY AND FUNCTIONAL EQUIVALENCE IN EXTENDED REFERENCE

12.3.1 A survey of items of extended reference in English and German

To give an idea of the number and variety of grammatical as well as lexical items used for extended reference in English and German, I have compiled a list (see Appendix) which must, however, be thought of as open-ended. The classification and the grouping together of English and German items is based on formal criteria. It does not reflect semantic and pragmatic equivalence or identical distribution in terms of frequency, stylistic value or discourse strategy. Those items which I consider rare, formal or at the limits of grammaticalness are put in parentheses.

12.3.2 Evidence for functional equivalence

The basic criterion for bringing together these diverse structures is the function they have in common at the level of discourse organization: they all serve the purpose of bundling up information given in what precedes or, less frequently, in what follows as single entities. This functional equivalence is reflected on the level of 'langue' and 'parole' and in the comparison of languages.

12.3.2.1 Evidence on the level of 'langue'
In the system of the language, transformational relations can be established, for example, between elliptical and non-elliptical structures or between a sequence of two sentences one of which contains the demonstrative *this* or *that* and a complex sentence with a sentential relative clause.

12.3.2.2 Evidence on the level of 'parole'
In the process of communication itself, different referential strategies are sometimes used subsequently. One reason may be the necessity for repair (a term adopted from Schegloff *et al.* 1977). It is either the hearer who initiates a repair sequence by asking for clarification, or the speaker who judges an expression not explicit enough and corrects himself immediately. The most frequent pattern is to replace a closed system item by a single or complex lexical item or even an embedded clause.

Self-initiated repair might be illustrated by examples such as the following. This type of structure is sometimes called 'right dislocation' and it cannot be denied that it is no longer a spontaneous mechanism of repair, but a fully grammaticalized structure.

(5) Ich habe gesagt: Ich verstehe dich nicht, verstehe nicht, kann nicht verstehen! DAS währte eine herrliche und große Weile lang, daß ihr nicht verstanden wurdet und selbst nicht verstandet . . .

I have said: I don't understand you, don't understand, can't understand! THAT persisted for a fine long while that you were not understood and yourselves didn't understand . . .

Other-initiated repair takes the form of a wh-question answered by a rephrasing of the closed-system reference item in lexical terms. The following example is particularly interesting because the hearer's request for clarification triggers the *ad hoc* coining of a complex lexical item.

(6) (NB: only the English version is given which follows the German original closely; only the dialogue is extracted from the narrative.)

Doctor: 'Hallo, here we are again'

Patient: 'What's happened?'

Doctor: 'On a clear stretch of road you crashed into the parapet of a bridge.'

Patient: 'I recognized her too late. All of a sudden she was sitting in the middle of the roadway . . .'

Doctor: 'Whom are you talking about?'

Patient: 'The cat'

Doctor: 'Indeed. It was all the fault of a cat?'

Patient: 'I should have run her over, then I'd have got peace.'

Doctor: 'Peace? From what?'

Patient: 'Why, from her!'

Doctor: 'Calm down . . . Funny business, this.
How long has THIS been bothering you?

Patient: 'What?'

Doctor: 'Well, THIS . . . CAT-COMPLEX.'

12.3.2.3 *Evidence from contrastive linguistics*

One potential point of criticism against my approach might be, I think, that what I called nominal and verbal realization of extended reference should not be treated together. As a matter of fact, there is evidence for equivalence relations of nominal and verbal constructions across languages in general and concerning extended reference in particular. In German the verbal realization type does exist, but it hardly ever occurs without a nominal reference item such as *das*, *es* or *so* which accompany the proverbs *machen* and *tun* or an auxiliary. This latter combination can, however, substitute for non-stative verbs only. As a consequence, extended reference expressed verbally in English is often rendered by a nominal pro-form in German whether this is the only translation possible or the one preferred.

(7) 'It's pleasant', said Mr. Bigger, relenting at last, 'to talk to somebody who really knows about painting. So few people DO.'

'Es ist ein Genuß', sagte Herr Bigger und ließ sich endlich erweichen, 'mit jemanden zu sprechen, der wirklich etwas von Malerei versteht. Das ist bei so wenig Menschen der Fall.'

12.4 SELECTED PROBLEMS OF EXTENDED REFERENCE IN ENGLISH AND GERMAN

12.4.1 Demonstrative items

A distinction that appears to be particularly subtle is the one between *this* and *that* in English. It is often drawn on the basis of the contrast of spatial proximity/non-proximity which is reinterpreted in terms of the temporal dimension, of location in the universe of discourse, or even of 'emotional' (Lakoff 1974: 346) or 'empathetic' (Lyons 1977: 677) deixis (cf. Halliday and Hasan 1976: 60; Lyons 1977: 668 f.). This leads then to the following conclusions: *this* tends to refer to what the speaker himself has said previously (Halliday and Hasan 1976: 60; Lakoff 1974: 346, 349) or to what only he himself but not his interlocutor knows (Fillmore 1971: 71); whereas *that* distances the speaker from what he or others have said (Lakoff 1974: 350) and is excluded from forward-pointing (Fillmore 1971: 71; Lakoff 1974: 350; Halliday and Hasan 1976: 68–70). Style and register certainly account for part of the patterns of usage (Halliday and Hasan 1976: 61); basically *this* seems to be more formal (Leech and Svartvik 1975: 38; Lakoff 1974: 349).

A comparison of the respective German and English demonstrative items raises many problems. In German, there is a threefold distinction between *dies—das—jenes*; the latter can, however, be neglected here because it seems to be confined to discrete reference. But even if we are left with the dual contrast *dies—das*, we cannot identify it with the seemingly parallel distinction in English. Generally speaking, *dies* is less frequent than English *this* and, more definitely than its English counterpart, belongs to a formal register. The criterion of proximity, whether in the literal or in the figurative sense, plays only a minor part in German. What seems to hold for both is that they are the standard forms for cataphoric reference.

I cannot go into further detail here; the only thing I should like to draw attention to is a problem of translation. The German pro-form *das* requires a choice between English *this* or *that*. The same holds for the adverbial pro-forms where, despite the superficial contrast between a *hier*-type and a *da*-type, the semantic distinction is almost neutralized. In the following examples German *das* was rendered by *this* in the English versions of the narratives.

(8) (NB: quoted fully in (6))

Wie lange haben Sie DAS schon?—Was?—Na, diesen Katzenkomplex.

How long has THIS been bothering you? What? Well this cat-complex.

(9) Also, Tatsache, sag ich, nu wüßt ich ja doch mal ganz gern, warum Sie mir DAS ALLES so haarklein erzählen.

Well, frankly, I say, now I'd dearly like to know why you've told me ALL THIS in such minute detail.

I do not want to maintain that the item *that* would have been impossible; on the other hand, *this*, with its connotation of shared interest and attention, seems to suit the communicative intention of the speaker in the narrative much better. Significantly, however, I found only two instances of *this* in the translations of the respective passages done by ten German students. As was shown in an empirical study by Stemmer 1981, extended reference, especially the adequate use of *this* and *it*, presents considerable problems to German learners.

12.4.2 Relative clause links

A question not dealt with in most text-based studies including Halliday and Hasan's *Cohesion in English* is the parallelism between complex sentences and sequences of sentences. An instance of this is the relationship between sentential relative clauses and independent clauses containing a demonstrative item (Quirk, Greenbaum, Leech and Svartvik 1972: 873). Evidence from short stories and from everyday conversation suggests that relative clause links with extended reference are definitely more frequent in English than in German and do not connote a formal register either. In my corpus most of these English *which*'s were rendered by German demonstratives. On the other hand, the relative clause link may be a potential translation for a German pro-form.

(10) Bestanden, Jan, nicht, du hast doch bestanden? (. . .) Bestanden, fragt sie abermals, und er DARAUF: mit Auszeichnung.

You've passed, haven't you, Jan, of course you've passed? (. . .) Passed? she reiterates *to which* he rejoins: with distinction.

12.4.3 Implicit reference

Quite often, extended reference is not signalled explicitly—a phenomenon I prefer to call implicit reference rather than ellipsis. I do not follow Halliday and Hasan's terminology here. Their classification of types of ellipsis accounts well for the structures of English, but can hardly be transferred to other languages. I suggest restricting the term 'ellipsis' to omission of parts of the verbal group in its narrow sense, where there are true structural slots which are not filled occasionally. Implicit reference occurs in different contexts; the degree of structural boundness is variable. It may fall within a verb's frame of valency. As studies in the theory of valency have shown, it is difficult to establish how many and which obligatory, optional or free 'players'—as the nominal groups came to be called—a verb may have. As a consequence, it is problematic to detect reference realized by zero. Extended reference may also depend on a preposition, but here again it is not easy to decide whether some reference item has been omitted, or whether the preposition has shifted into the category of adverbs. Finally, minimal responses with *yes/no* or modal elements such as *probably*, *quite* etc. may be looked upon as cases of implicit reference to a piece of preceding discourse.

A problem of particular interest from a contrastive point of view is that of implicit vs. explicit reference in object position. Grammars for the use of the non-native speaker usually contain lists of verbs after which no pro-form is used to refer back to a preceding clause or string of clauses. This means relegating the problem to the lexicon. By contrast, Halliday and Hasan (1976: 221) provide a syntactic explanation for the deletability of pro-sentential forms, namely, that report clauses—but not fact clauses—may be realized by zero. What is needed, I think, is both a description of individual verbs in terms of syntactic and semantic valency and a discourse-based approach which throws light on the relations between different types of antecedents (or maybe 'postcedents'!) and different reference signals including zero.

In the lists of verbs said to allow the omission of a sentential object we frequently find *tell*. In vain, however, do we look for a systematic comparison of *tell* + zero vs. *tell* + *this/that/it/so*, whether in grammars or dictionaries. I now cite some examples of the verb *tell* and its German translations, or vice versa, in order to give an idea of the complexity of the problem, especially from the point of view of contrastive linguistics and language learning.

(11) 'Yes,' Uncle Gavin said, 'why didn't you tell me ø?' 'I didn't recognize it myself,' Quick said, 'it wasn't until I heard your jury was hung and by one man, that I associated the names.' 'Names?' Uncle Gavin said, 'what na- Never mind. Just TELL IT.'

'Ja,' bestätigte Onkel Gavin, 'warum haben Sie's mir nicht GESAGT?' 'Hab's selber nicht begriffen,' sagte Quick, 'erst als ich gehört habe, daß Ihre Geschworenen festhingen, und zwar wegen dem einen Mann—erst da hab' ich die Namen in Zusammenhang gebracht!' 'Die Namen?' rief Onkel Gavin, 'was für Na- Einerlei! ERZÄHLEN Sie mir ø!'

(12) (Context: a coyote has come to the village and killed a turkey.)

Mark Coopers (. . .) TOLD Franz Lazamian ABOUT IT.

Mark Coopers (. . .) BENACHRICHTIGTE ø Franz Lazamian.

(13) Unser Jan wird's schaffen. Ich hab's euch VORAUSGESAGT.

Our Jan will manage that. I TOLD you SO in advance.

(14) Warum sind Sie dann zu mir gekommen? Nur um mir DAS zu SAGEN?

Why have you come to me then? Only to TELL me THAT?

12.4.4 Lexical items

The use of lexical items as well as of the concomitant phoric modifiers with reference to larger stretches of text has been given little attention in discourse studies. In Halliday and Hasan (1976: 72) there is a brief hint at general nouns functioning in this way. These quasi-closed-system items do in fact play an important part in establishing extended reference. The equivalence of the latter and of pro-forms becomes apparent in translations whether this transposition is an optional or necessary one.

(15) Toll, sag ich, wie Sie DAS ALLES so im Kopf haben.

Marvellous, I say, how you carry ALL THAT STUFF in your head.

(16) There are two new guests arriving this afternoon. I have only received the letter acquainting me with THE FACT this morning.

Heute Nachmittag treffen zwei neue Gäste ein. Ich habe den Brief, der ES mir mitteilt, erst heute früh bekommen.

An important instrument for activating and condensing given information are all sorts of nominalization:

(17) (Context: a child has been waiting for his father in front of a bar for several hours.)

He was a boy who had been toughened by hard times of all kinds, and THIS WAITING in the street for his father wasn't going to be too much for him.

Es war ein Junge, der durch Härten aller Art zäh geworden war und DAS WARTEN auf der Straße bis der Vater käme, würde ihm nicht übermäßig viel anhaben können.

General nouns and nominalizations are the only instances of lexical extended reference that can be distinguished on formal grounds. To delimit in some way the class of lexical items that may function in this way is virtually impossible. All the items in question have a categorizing effect, but at least two types should be distinguished: categorization may apply on a text internal level of abstraction.

(18) Louise outlived her husband. He caught his death of cold one day ... It was wonderful that she managed to survive THE SHOCK.

Louise überlebte ihren Mann. Er holte sich eines Tages den Tod durch eine Erkältung ... Es war bewundernswert, wie sie es fertigbrachte, DIESEN SCHLAG zu überstehen.

It would be interesting to study not only the use of the lexical items, but also of the phoric modifiers. Significantly, no theory of the definite article has, to my knowledge, accounted for these cases in a systematic way.

Categorization may, on the other hand, apply on a meta-communicative level of abstraction. The distinction is neutralized in pro-forms so that a translator may think it necessary to make it clear that reference is on the meta-communicative level, as in the following example. Whether the translation is in fact adequate I do not want to question.

(19) Er, anmaßend: Sie meinen, Sie hätten nicht das richtige Verständnis dafür. Ich, ruhig: DAS dürfte auf Ihre Bemühungen eher zutreffen.

He, presumptuously: You mean you were incapable of fully understanding it. I, coolly: THAT remark might more properly fit your
endeavours.

12.5 CONCLUSION

It has been one of my aims in this paper to argue for a concept of 'extended
reference' as opposed to 'discrete reference', a concept defined functionally at
the level of discourse organization. A more detailed theoretical study would
have to tackle such problems as the factors determining the interpretation of
the reference items and the scope of the antecedents (or postcedents). An
interesting question to examine would be how the primary function of
bundling up and categorizing continuous information into handy chunks
shades into secondary functions such as delimiting and subdividing longer
texts, underlining the turn-taking structure, commenting on locution and
illocution of previous utterances, meta-communicative evaluation etc.
Another aim has been to draw attention to interlingual contrasts in discourse
structure and in particular to a complex of problems which has hardly ever
been treated. I think it has become clear that here most of the work still
remains to be done.

APPENDIX

A survey of extended reference in English and German

A: Nominal realization of extended reference

(1) Closed system items

(a) Simple items
    this that here there it so thus not   *dies das (jenes) hier da es eines alles*

(b) Simple items with modifier
    all this all that it all (this much) (that   *all dies all das soviel so etwas*
    much) (so much)

(c) Complex items
    preposition + *this that it*   (preposition + *das (dies jenes)*)
    (hereby herein hereof hereupon here-   *hieran hierauf hierdurch hierfür hier-*
    with)   *gegen hiermit hiernach hierin hierüber*
                                      hierunter hiervon hierzu . . .

    (thereafter thereby therefore therein   *daran darauf daraufhin daraus dabei*
    (after) thereof thereto thereupon . . .)   *dadurch dafür dagegen daher damit*
    . . .   *danach daneben darin darüber darum*
                                      darunter davon davor dazu . . .
                                      deshalb deswegen demnach
                                      infolgedessen trotzdem überdies
                                      insofern insoweit . . .

(d) Relative clause links
which as
preposition + *which*
(whereat whereby wherein whereof
whereto whereupon wherewith) which
fact which matter . . . a fact which a
thing which

was wie
(preposition + *was*)
woran worauf woraus wobei wodurch
wofür wogegen womit wonach worin
worüber worunter wovon wovor wozu
. . . weshalb weswegen eine Tatsache
die (etwas das)

(e) Implicit reference
— depending on a verb   =
— depending on a preposition   =
— independent, along with   =
    response particles

(f) Unclassified items
this way that way like this like that
likewise the same the foregoing the
following the above above below
. . .

das Gleiche dergleichen dasselbe das
Ganze das Vorausgehende das
Folgende Folgendes oben unten
. . .

(2) *Lexical item + phoric modifier*
phoric modifiers:
the this that such the same the whole
the former the latter the first the last

der dieser jener so ein solch derartig
derselbe der gleiche der ganze ersterer
letzterer der erste der letzte

lexical items:
formal classifications: general nouns (quasi-closed-system—
nominalizations—other simple items
semantic classification: categorization on text internal level—categorization
on meta-communicative level

B: Verbal Realization of extended reference
(1) proverb + *this that it so*
(2) ellipsis in the verbal group
    (including pro-infinitive)

proverb (including modal auxilia-
ries) + *das dies es*
Ø

13 Discourse Error Analysis

Rod Haden

Colchester English Study Centre/University of Essex (now Adam Mickiewicz University, Poznań)

In this chapter I will discuss the pursuit of Contrastive Analysis and Error of Analysis 'beyond the sentence', taking into account cultural as well as linguistic factors, but in particular concentrating on the discourse level, under which term I include all aspects of text organization above the sentence.

I will begin by discussing the practice of Contrastive Analysis (CA) and Error Analysis (EA); I will then say something about approaches to Discourse Analysis and Text Linguistics and I will conclude by looking at some data of two kinds: contrastive data and examples of actual foreign-learner errors.

13.1 CONTRASTIVE ANALYSIS

Increasingly of late, stress has been laid on the need for a contrastive analysis which contrasts communicative use of different languages, and which not only asks in what ways does language x differ from language y but also in what ways does the use of language x differ from the use of language y. This is advocated, for example, by researchers working with CA projects in the University of Jyvaskälä in Finland, in the Adam Mickiewicz University in Poznań, and in the Serbo-Croatian-English Contrastive Project in Zagreb. An important aspect of this tendency is the greater attention paid to CA at a text-linguistic/discourse level, the central concern also in Reinhardt Hartmann's work towards the development of a theory of 'Contrastive Textology'.

As early as 1968 at the XIXth Georgetown Round Table Meeting on Linguistics and Language Studies, whose theme was Contrastive Linguistics and its pedagogical implications, it was stated by Lado that we cannot adequately compare two languages at the sentence level. Support for this view comes from Di Pietro 1971, who quotes a recommendation of the Fédération Internationale de Professeurs de Langues Vivantes (meeting in Yugoslavia also in 1968) that 'CA should be undertaken beyond the sentence level into discourse structures, in semantics and on the socio-cultural and psycho-linguistic levels', to which he does, however, add the caveat that 'as for

*I am indebted to Jeffrey Ellis, Carl James and Jean Ure who, with their comments and suggestions, helped me to rid the first version of this chapter of some of its defects.

discourse structure, much more theoretical ground must be gained before a CA of language-specific patterns can be profitably attempted'.

In the decade since those words were written a good deal of the relevant theoretical ground has been covered. In particular, progress has been made on the study of discourse structure, though application to contrastive linguistic study and specifically in contrastive analysis is just beginning. One cannot point to a vast amount of progress, but some has been made and there have been several attempts to widen the scope of CA, some of which I would now like to consider.

Some research projects in this area accept Politzer's (1972) view of the need to link contrastive language analysis ultimately to a 'contrastive cultural analysis' (adumbrated in Lado 1957). This poses formidable problems since, as Dimitrjević 1977 points out, 'Before a contrastive analysis of two cultures can be made both of them must be accurately described and analysed using the same methodological approach'—assuredly no mean task. It is certain, though, that 'negative transfer' of cultural knowledge is common. This may cause the kind of 'sociopragmatic failure' described by Thomas 1983, for example, through a foreign speaker's ignorance of what questions it is considered proper to ask in a given society, or his deviant assessment of size of imposition, social distance etc. It may involve such non-linguistic activities as kissing or hand-shaking or else the kind of much more complex shared knowledge between interlocutors which can be crucial to the coherence of a discourse—that, for instance, in a particular society stamps are sold at tobacconists, milk may be left on doorsteps etc.

For Riley 1981 these considerations would fall within the 'ethno-discourse' level—those sets of presuppositions which speakers impose upon the reality their language dissects'—an area where directly contrastive studies are lacking. The cultural presuppositions on which coherence depends, he points out, involve both knowledge of events and knowledge of the world.

Especially important among cultural phenomena will be those non-verbal behaviours which realize communicative acts and must, as Riley 1981 says, be regarded as having an illocutionary function because of their role in normal interaction—head-nodding for agreeing, commanding (by beckoning to come) etc. It seems clear that in a full contrastive study non-verbal means of communication must find their place. Just as comparisons may be made, on functional grounds, across linguistic levels, on occasion too they may have to be of verbal with non-verbal signals (cf. the description of the French exclamation 'bof!' as 'a verbal shrug'); and this must be an important factor in contrastive communication studies. Thus, although as linguists we must recognize and concentrate on a clearly demarcated verbal aspect to communication, these non-verbal aspects cannot be ignored because of the way they interact with and affect verbal communication.

In the Finnish–English Contrastive Project an attempt is being made to 'consider language users' communicative competence as a whole'. Learning another language is viewed as expansion of the learner's communicative competence (in Halliday's terms, it is 'learning how to mean' in another code). So CA must be expanded to include sociolinguistic and psycholinguistic data;

also 'the systems [of the two languages] will have to be brought side by side in relevant contexts for making observations on parameters which affect the intelligibility of messages in communicative situations' (Sajavaara 1977).

Similar preoccupations are to be found in the Poznan Contrastive Linguistic publications—for example, in Janicki's (1977) plea for a Pedagogical Contrastive Sociolinguistics, involving the construction of a 'grammar of social interaction' alongside a linguistic grammar ('a finite set of rules on the basis of which an infinite number of social behaviours would be generated', incorporating some such notion as Halliday's 'situation types' and Grimshaw's (1973) 'interactional universals').

More amenable to constrastive analysis, no doubt, is the structure of conversational openings, as undertaken at the University of Bochum and discussed by James 1980.

In their work Riley and his colleagues at the University of Nancy II insist on the complex nature of communicative acts and the importance of a pragmatic dimension in CA. Riley 1981 describes and illustrates a tripartite division of the communicative situation into formal structure, illocutionary structure and interactive structure. He shows how aspects of role, status, directivity and formality can be objectively described in terms of interactional behaviour and the discourse privileges of the participants (convincingly enough at least for the example he gives).

There is, then, no lack of conviction as to the important role a more extended CA can play in improving foreign language teaching, though at present there is little agreement how best to proceed.

13.1.2 Criticisms of Contrast Analysis

Perhaps we could dispense with what Di Pietro 1982 calls 'the customary list of limitations and defences of CA', but I will say something about two criticisms levelled against CA.

The first is that of Lee 1968, who objects that: 'A language is not a collection of separate and self-sufficient parts. The parts are mutually dependent and mutually determinative. They determine each other's use and meaning.' But the possible implication that CA should only be undertaken if we are in a position to describe 'whole languages' and compare complete descriptions is surely undesirable. Depending on what one would agree to accept as a 'complete description', such a requirement would postpone usable CAs for decades at the very least. And if we consider the extended scope of much contemporary CA this criticism becomes even more pointed.

I accept the contrary view, expressed by Catford, also at the Georgetown meeting: 'It is impossible to say how two complex systems such as languages contrast without first reducing these systems to manageable sub-systems'. A more valid criticism of CA is the problem of the lack of established criteria of comparability, the lack of suitable *tertium comparationis*. For applied purposes translation equivalence is the obvious candidate, in spite of its generally recognized theoretical inadequacy, and: 'Two constructions can be regarded as equivalent when one is an optimal translation of the other' (Marton 1968). Now this clearly depends on a consensus among bilingual (and bicultural) individuals and is often fraught with difficulty, especially where extensive culture shifts are involved. It is nonetheless true that for a wide variety of practical purposes the possibility of such a consensus can, indeed must, be assumed and relied on.

Though interesting attempts to make use of a putative common deep-structure have been made, large-scale success for this approach does not seem to be forthcoming, though it seems that the way forward to a theoretically satisfactory *tertium comparationis* must be in terms of something like an abstract meaning structure of some sort. In the meantime, though, in my view it is unhelpful, to say the least, to talk about differences between languages as being 'merely surface'.

In what follows I will take it for granted that a full CA would incorporate cultural data and that, although a strong form of the CA hypothesis may be untenable, CA of the kind Schachter calls 'a priori' is nonetheless of considerable importance in Applied Linguistics, not least for the possibilities it gives of prediction of learners' receptive behaviour as well as their expressive behaviour, of 'covert' as well as 'overt' errors (in the sense of Corder 1973), of potential as well as actual errors, and of the likelihood of 'avoidance'[1] strategies.

13.2 ERROR ANALYSIS

A number of works insist on the importance of sources of error other than interference from the learner's L_1, for example, Richards 1974 (and, indeed, some have overstated this importance)[2] so that error analysis (EA) can be considered to complement CA, primarily by casting light on sources of error other than L_1 interference. Of course, it also tests the predictions of CA, especially so far as expressive errors are concerned.

George (1972, cited by Chesterman 1977) surmises that about one-third of errors of adult learners can be explained as L_1 interference. We may assume that this excludes from consideration receptive errors, and my impression is that if errors were classified according to linguistic levels quite a different picture would emerge at some levels and in some particular areas—for instance, the greater part of the errors of textual cohesion and 'connection' that I have come across are apparently due to 'negative transfer' from the L_1 (they are interlingual errors in Richards's 1974 sense).

George's definition is 'a form unwanted by the teacher or course designer', and this is suitable in the classroom with a teacher in control (although what is 'unwanted' may at times include correct but overcomplicated forms!).

But such considerations are premature before we face the problem of definition. What IS an error?

I would certainly not agree with Angelis 1975 in treating as errors the omission of non-obligatory 'connectives' in examples like:

(1) We stayed in LA for 3 days. We rested from our trip. We visited Disneyland.
(2) It was early. I decided to read the newspaper. Then I went to bed.

Are not these examples of avoidance rather than error? And surely the examples of 'failure to respond' which Allwright includes among 'error events' represent the extreme case of avoidance rather than examples of error! (Though, as he points out, the judgement of what constitutes this failure depends on the teacher and tends to be more favorable to better students.)

Corder 1973 distinguishes lapses and mistakes from errors. Lapses are 'slips, false starts and confusions of structure which result in an unacceptable utterance' (and which, in the case of the foreign learner, may be indistinguishable from 'errors', at least initially). Not infrequently they involve slips of cohesion in spoken language, of which examples are not uncommon in the media, which, if produced by foreign students would be likely to be regarded as evidence of an idiosyncratic transitional competence. Recent *Radio 4* examples are:

(3) Not all political commentators concentrate on these two stories however. SUCH were . . . [i.e. some who did not] . . . The money will go into a trust fund and the interest USED to pay a subsidy. [intra-sentential cohesion in the latter case]

The term 'mistakes' Corder reserves for inappropriate use—selection of the wrong variety—and this too is not so uncommon among native speakers. True errors, like lapses, also result in an unacceptable utterance but are rare among adult native speakers.

The distinction between 'lapses' and 'errors' is important: we should not wish to try to draw pedagogical conclusions from every unacceptable utterance our students produce. But if we are considering errors from the discourse perspective of language in use in situation, it seems that Corder's category of 'mistakes' is a particular, rather important class of discourse error which I personally would not wish to differentiate terminologically.

For present purposes I will consider as instances of error utterances and parts of utterances which are unacceptable or inappropriate in some way in terms of the target language norms in relation to the foreign speaker's intention, and which he either cannot correct spontaneously or which he is liable to repeat. They may be 'expressive' or 'receptive' (Corder 1973). Within the scope of this definition come what Thomas 1983 calls instances of 'pragmalinguistic failure', such as misapprehensions about illocutionary force, which she expressly dissociates from the notion of 'error' (as entailing 'probable' rather than categorical rules'). The justification for considering such instances to be errors is that they can be 'systematic' (Corder 1973) rather than fortuitous, and clear cases where the speaker's performance fails to conform with his intentions, or else where he fails to understand what a speaker intended (a high proportion of 'receptive errors' fall into this category), are common enough.

In terms of Johansson's (1978) judgements of error gravity, these errors would contravene the first, most important criterion: that of communicative efficiency. At the same time it is clear, though, that here 'lapses', especially 'receptive' ones, are fairly common even among native speakers, and indeed that genuinely ambiguous utterances may sometimes be involved. This fact does not invalidate the general principle; nor does the fact that in some of the relevant areas, such as illocutionary structure and register study, our linguistic descriptions are still in need of considerable refinement.

Quite apart from this question of definition there is that of recognition of error—obviously a most important matter, and one where consideration of discourse factors has always been to the fore. An important category of error here to which I have already alluded is that of 'covert' errors. Corder 1973 gives the example of a learner's utterance 'I want to know the English', where, however 'the context showed that his interest lay not in the people but in their language'. Various plausible linguistic contexts with subsequent development of the discourse could lead to this particular error being discovered. One possibility is that of immediate cohesive reference, for instance, the next sentence being 'It is such a useful language' rather than 'They are such a strange people'. Another possibility is a gradual semantic development whereby the speaker's complete indifference to the English is made (more or less) clear.

On the other hand, it is also quite likely that such an error will pass unnoticed and consequent misunderstanding may persist, especially where no a priori prediction of the kind produced by CA is available.

13.3 DISCOURSE ANALYSIS AND TEXT LINGUISTICS

The terms 'text' and 'discourse' have, of course, been used to make a number of different distinctions within the general area of suprasentential linguistics; for instance, for some people it is a matter of spoken or written language (written text versus spoken discourse).

For present purposes I am following Ellis 1976 and Halliday and Hasan 1976 in treating these terms as synonymous, and by 'discourse error' in my title I refer to all kinds of error in text organization 'beyond the sentence'. There are, however, a number of precedents for using derivatives of these terms to make a distinction between textual structure, theme and information structure and cohesion, on the one hand, and discourse structure which is concerned with speech acts, with the ways in which people put language to use, in Labov's terms with WHAT IS DONE rather than WHAT IS SAID, on the other.

It will be convenient to refer to this latter as 'discourse structure', though I do not intend to imply thereby any distinction between the terms 'text' and 'discourse' of the same kind as is often made between 'sentence' and 'utterance', where the reasons for such a distinction are certainly much more compelling.

It is in terms of 'discourse structure' in this sense that the most promising attempts to incorporate socio-cultural settings into linguistic research have been made, though Johns 1980 is surely right to warn against 'a tendency for functional labels to proliferate in the absence of a clear theoretical basis for establishing a hierarchy of functions and for distinguishing their realizations in text'. In this connection it may be mentioned that Riley 1981 points out that separate analysis of illocutionary structure and interactive structure in terms of two different types of act makes the former much simpler in that few different types of act need to be distinguished. It may be that further development of this approach will point the way forward, but a great deal remains to be done for the establishment of the kind of functional hierarchy Johns mentions, to say nothing of the vast question of distinguishing realizations in text.

Ellis discusses the notion 'text' under three headings: firstly, 'demarcation of texts'—from the theoretical point of view a far from straightforward matter, though for applied purposes a 'text' in this sense can often be equated with some objectively defined unit such as Sinclair and Coulthard's 'lesson' or Burton's (1981) 'interaction'; secondly, 'having the quality of being TEXT, the aspect or function of language that constitutes this'—this involves what was referred to as 'textual structure' above; and thirdly, 'having the structure of a text'—what we have decided here to refer to as 'discourse structure'.

Relevant under all three headings is the concept of register, as Ellis points out. An essential characteristic of a text and usually a factor in its unity is the register used ('every test is an instance of a register': Hasan 1977), and a change of register will usually involve a change of text (though the new one may be embedded in the first, as when a lecturer breaks off his exposition to complain, perhaps in more colloquial language, about someone talking during his lecture).[3]

Register is the kind of variety involved in what Corder refers to as 'mistakes', as I pointed out earlier. To avoid these, he suggests, it is necessary 'to make an appropriate selection of features at all levels'; he even considers slang with a foreign accent to be a 'stylistic mistake'. While in some situations and for many people this may be so, it seems to me an exaggeration. Surely between work-mates and fellow students, indeed, with anyone with whom a solidary relation is felt, it is perfectly normal so long as co-occurence rules (Ervin-Tripp 1972) are respected (or only contravened on purpose for special effect). Where these rules are not respected or where the register used is at variance with the situation (intentional special effects aside), we are justified in speaking of error, although in terms of error gravity such errors are perhaps not very serious ones. I believe that in view of the relation between register and text/discourse it is also reasonable to view them as 'discourse errors'.

13.4 LINGUISTIC DATA

I would now like to consider some linguistic data, both contrastive predictions and actual occurrences of error in terms of the concepts discussed above, in the hope that the previous discussion will serve in some measure to clarify the data.

13.4.1 Cultural background

Our starting point was the importance of a cultural dimension in contrastive studies which has clear relevance to language teaching. It is not, however, necessary or appropriate for language teaching purposes to extend the concept of error and error analysis into this area; it will not tell us anything about the language teaching process or language acquisition strategies. Obviously to the greatest possible extent, knowledge of the specific cultural presuppositions on which coherence may depend needs to be judiciously incorporated into teaching materials, as do those culture-specific gestures which may form an integral part of a communication.

In 'sociopragmatic' matters Thomas rightly insists that prescriptivism is not appropriate. It is not up to the teacher to aim to change learners' systems of beliefs; (s)he should rather try to heighten and refine their meta-pragmatic awareness so that they can express themselves as they choose to, being able to be rude, for instance, by design rather than by accident (Thomas 1983: 91).

13.4.2 Discourse-structure errors

Most errors in this area involve some misapprehension about an intended illocutionary act and are of special interest as they are not uncommon and have been neglected on the whole.

Of course, genuinely ambiguous cases of this kind are fairly common; a well-known one given by Sinclair and Coulthard 1975 is that of a teacher's interrogative ('elicitation') 'Why are you laughing?' being misunderstood by a native-speaker pupil as 'directive' (to stop laughing). And a similar case from my own EFL experience is the following:

(4) —He is in prison
    —Why is he in prison?
    —Because I can see the bars.

(in the illustration). In Halliday and Hasan's (1976) terms this is an indirect response of the 'commentary' type instead of the expected direct response ('—Because he kidnapped someone').

These two examples are cases of either genuine ambiguity or, perhaps, 'receptive lapse'. A clear example of a non-native-speaker error in this area is Richards's (1975) example of an exchange in a Singapore shop:

(5) —Hello, how are you today?
    —Thank you and the same to you.

In the absence of any relevant contrastive data, the source of this error could be considered to be either L_1 interference (though this seems unlikely) or else over-generalization (assignment of the first utterance to the wrong (secondary delicacy) class of 'greeting').

Contrastive study suggests many other possibilities. Let us consider a few: (a) Riley gives the example of conditional clauses in French, Swedish and English. In French and Swedish, but not in English, such constructions, as well as being used to 'hypothesize', are used to request confirmation (['Si je suis prêt? [C'est bien ce que tu viens de me demander']) and also to suggest ('Si on allait au cinéma ce soir?'). Errors arising from L_1 interference, both receptive (for English learners of French who might remain unaware that a suggestion had been made) and expressive (for French learners of English), are clearly possible here and in the latter case would probably be of the covert variety, being interpretable as an unfinished construction.

(b) An important difference exists between English and French, and doubtless other languages, in the expression of what may perhaps be provisionally called the illocutionary act of 'reciprocating', as the following French examples show:

(6) —Je t'aime bien.   —Moi aussi.
    —Je t'ai vu en ville ce matin.   —Moi aussi, mais j'étais pressé.
    —Je t'emmerde!   —Moi aussi.

(cf. English: '—I like you.' and '—And I like YOU', an instance of a rather more straightforward cohesive relationship (where such elliptical replies as 'Me too' and 'I do too' would mean 'I like myself' (at least in my idiolect).)

English learners are susceptible to receptive errors here,—perhaps taking it that their interlocutor is being facetious.

(c) English, like French and Russian, has more than one type of interrogative construction. However Dubois-Charlier 1975 points out that in expressing surprise at finding a child drinking something in the kitchen just after a meal only an 'intonation question' is appropriate in French ('Tu as encore soif?'). I believe the same would be true of an 'intonation question' in Russian. Other interrogative constructions would be 'real' questions. In English in the same circumstances, 'You're still thirsty?' and 'Are you still thirsty?' can both be appropriately used.

Analogous, but more complex English examples are given in van der Brook *et al.* 1980, a discussion of the use of appropriate question forms dependent on the amount of presupposition of a 'yes' or 'no' answer; inappropriate uses are classed as errors.

(d) In Polish it is possible to reply to a question with the question 'Czy ja wiem?' (lit. 'Do I know?'). For native speakers of some other languages there is a distinct possibility of a receptive error here, since this reply is not peevish or impolite, being more or less equivalent to 'nie mam pojęcia' ('I've no idea'). The reaction might be similar to that with Thomas's examples with 'konečno' in Russian, which is used as an 'enthusiastic affirmative' without the gloss its equivalent ('of course') would be likely to bear in English ('What a stupid question!') (Thomas 1983: 102).

(e)The Russian 'kažetsja' ('it seems'/'I think') is not only used 'to deliver considered judgements', but also its use implies that the speaker is vouching for the statement made (whether or not 'to me' ('mne') is expressed). Russians not infrequently use 'it seems' in English (rather than, say, 'I think') and often erroneously, since 'it seems' implies that the speaker does not vouch for the statement made, that he has it from a third person, and, in many cases, that he does not believe it at all.

(f) The above examples concern differences in the detail of realization of particular illocutionary acts. Riley gives an example of a difference in the actual elements of discourse structure: in English and Swedish a compliment may be followed by an expression of thanks, in French (as in Thai, according to Richards and Sukwiwat 1983 it may not. An analogous case is acceptance of an offer which in English normally includes 'please', but which in French does not include 's'il vous plaît'.

(g) Languages can, of course, also vary in the explicit performative verbs that they possess. It is tempting here to contrast English, which, as Coulthard 1977 points out in his discussion of Austin's performative analysis, has no explicit performative verb 'to insult' (no 'I (hereby) insult you') with French, which has in 'Je t'emmerde!' something surely very like one!

These few examples must suffice to indicate the kind of data contrastive discourse-structure analysis may be expected to concern itself with. In Widdowson's terms they are matters of 'use' as opposed to 'usage', which are clearly no less frequently susceptible to 'negative transfer'.

13.4.3 Register errors

Register errors may involve either the inappropriateness of whole utterances to the situation or else failure to respect co-occurence rules of the kind described by Ervin-Tripp 1972. Examples of the former occur quite often in the subtitles of French films—for example, in the treatment of 'merde' as if it were the equivalent of a four-letter word. The latter type are perhaps more common among foreign learners, or at any rate they are more noticeable and more noticeably aberrant. An example I myself uttered some years ago is 'Que de gosses!', where, as I was told, there is incongruity between a formal expression of quantity and a slang lexical item.

Ervin-Tripp distinguishes between 'horizontal co-occurrence' involving lexical items (her example: 'How's it goin', your Eminence?') and 'vertical co-occurrence', where there is incongruity across linguistic levels—for instance, slang lexical items are used in a formal syntactic structure. The last French example is of this kind. Others might be: 'Que fous-tu?', 'Que fabriques-tu?', and an example from Corder 1973: 'Beware lest the dog tear the pants off you.'

In common with many other kinds of error, errors of register cannot always be readily categorized as intralingual or interlingual: in the former case we have the explanation of unjustified over-generalization of use from one situation to another which is different in some crucial way; in the latter case we have the explanation of wrongly assumed equivalence with some item in the L_1. These explanations do not appear to be mutually exclusive.

13.4.4 Information-focus errors

These are common in the spoken English of English learners of different nationalities:

(7) —A lot of people qualify as doctors every year. The problem is there's no places for THĔM.
    —It's quite incomparable between our schools and their SCHŎOLS.

Direct L_1 interference seems highly unlikely here and such errors appear to be a normal feature of 'transitional competence', albeit one very prone to fossilization.

13.4.5 Thematic-structure errors.

Examples of this category of error are not all that frequent. One occurs in the following written answer:

(8) (—How long ago did the weather become miserable?)
    —Nine days ago the weather became miserable.

which is clearly an intralingual error and clearly teaching-induced. On the other hand, an error in this area which is obviously due to negative interference from English is the following Russian example:

(9) Eto byl v 1958–om godu kogda Xruščev ukazal . . . [sic]

a clumsy attempt to translate an English 'theme predication' construction.

13.4.6 Cohesion errors

These are very common and are mostly due to L_1 interference, as in the case of English-speaking students' use in Russian of 'tak' ('so', 'in this way') for 'itak' ('(and) so' (conjunction)); or in French of 'il s'est passé (for 'ça s'est passé'). Some examples, though, are due to over-generalization of L_2 structure:

(10) They can talk some broken French, but not the standard ONE [French-speaker]

Le lendemain je suis allé chez un opticien pour en commander une nouvelle [sc. 'lentille']. Quand j'Y suis entré . . . [English-speaker]

The whole area of connectives, including Winter's (1977) 'lexical connectors', which have not here been given the attention they deserve in a contrastive study, is one where L_1 interference seems to account for many errors, for example, in written (English-speakers):

(11) Elle était assise sur un banc et sa concentration sur un journal l'empêchait de voir le chien. AINSI, elle ignorait que le chien n'était plus en vue.
Ces rochers abritaient une colline de vie marine, qui bien souvent attirait des enfants. EN VÉRITÉ, il y avait une petite fille dans les rochers. ['As a matter of fact . . .' (?)]

Some speakers show evidence of 'overindulgence' (Levenston 1971) in the use of connectives—an advanced learner of EFL introducing most of his sentences in a seminar presentation by 'now', and an English learner of French similarly making (over-) use of 'mais'.

A particularly interesting cohesive phenomenon from a contrastive point of view (if it IS a cohesive phenomenon; Halliday and Hasan 1976 count it as one, including it in clausal ellipsis) is the use of 'yes' and 'no'. Speakers of many languages, including Arabic and Russian, have a problem here due to L_1 interference, since in their languages the equivalents of these words mean, as it were, 'you are right/wrong' rather than 'answer positive/answer negative' as in English. There is considerable scope for receptive errors here: I have discovered, for example, Arabic-speaking learners of English thinking that the answer 'yes' to the two questions 'Are you coming?', 'Aren't you coming?' has opposite meanings. Productive errors are just as likely.

13.5 CONCLUSION

We have looked, then, at some of the kinds of discourse-level error and also some cases where contrastive data predict that such errors are likely to occur have been considered. These errors and potential errors have been categorized in terms of different aspects of textual organization and I have suggested that the predominant source of error will differ considerably from one category to another. This remains to be investigated more thoroughly.

In all that precedes the problem of error recognition looms large. This problem can be eased by wider and deeper contrastive analyses, and by large-scale studies of foreign-user errors. Thomas 1983 puts forward the view that 'pragmalinguistic failure' is a matter of contravention of 'highly conventionalized usage which can be taught quite straightforwardly as part of the grammar', and she discusses some ways in which this might be done. I am in complete agreement with Thomas here and it seems that the insights from CA and EA are crucial to this teaching.

On the question of error gravity, it was stated in Corder 1974 that 'referential' and 'textual' errors, since they interfere with communication, are much more serious than 'register' and 'social' errors, where more tolerance is possible. This is broadly true, assuming that his 'textual' is 'thematic structure' (the (fictitious?) example he gives is: 'Who is that man over there?— *John is'). Both his 'register' and his 'social' errors are errors of what is referred to here as 'register'. However, when we consider discourse-structure errors we find some examples where communication is impaired and others where something less serious happens (e.g. the speaker's attitude is misunderstood/misencoded). Cohesion errors, too, do not usually affect communicative efficiency, though I am sure there are many exceptions, one of which (misunderstanding of 'yes'/'no') has been mentioned. This area, too, one feels, would repay further study.

This chapter has been programmatic and exploratory, and its constant refrain seems to be the need for further research, but I hope that it has contributed in a small measure to pointing the way towards the extension and consolidation of CA and EA, and that it may be followed by some of the more detailed work which it finds lacking.

NOTES

1. The term is Schachter's 1974, though, as Johansson 1978 points out, Weinreich 1953 refers to the phenomenon: '. . . poverty of expression in the second language (i.e. exaggerated concentration on high-frequency forms and a propensity for circumlocution of difficult forms) is as a rule not recorded as a lack of proficiency, even though it is a result of interference.' I find unnecessary and confusing Johansson's use of the term 'covert error' in this connection (apparently covering both complete ignorance of particular forms and avoidance of their use because of uncertainty about them.

2. For example, Dulay and Burt 1972. They discuss errors in terms of 'two conflicting hypotheses': (1) that second-language learning errors result from first-language interference; and (2) that second-language learning errors will be similar to first-language developmental errors and do not result from negative transfer. But these are not really 'conflicting hypotheses' at all—they are alternative explanations either or BOTH of which may be relevant in a particular case of error.

3. For examples of register change within a text, see Ellis 1965, note 24.

Bibliography

Akinnaso, F. N. (1982), 'On the differences between spoken and written language', *Language and Speech*, **25**, 97–125.

Alatis, J. (ed.) (1968), *Report on the 19th Annual Round Table Meeting on Linguistics and Language Studies: Contrastive Linguistics*, Washington, D.C., Georgetown University Press.

Al-Kasimi, A. (1977), *Linguistics and Bilingual Dictionaries*, Leiden, Brill.

Allen, J. P. B and Corder, S. P. (eds) (1974), *Techniques in Applied Linguistics. The Edinburgh Course in Applied Linguistics III*, London, Oxford University Press.

Allwright, R. L. (1975), 'Problems in the study of the teacher's treatment of learner error', in Burt and Dulay (eds) (1975).

Altenberg, B. (1984), 'Causal linking in spoken and written English', *Studia Linguistica*, **38**, 20–69.

Angelis, P. J. (1975), 'Sentence combining, error analysis and the teaching of writing', in Burt and Dulay (eds) (1975).

Anscombe, G. E. M. (1975), 'Intention', *Proceedings of the Aristotelian Society*, **57**, 321–32.

Arndt, H. (1979), 'Some neglected types of speech function', in Petterson (ed.) (1979).

Arndt, H. (1982), 'An ordered inventory of communicative functions for general FLT', read at the Symposium on Communication in the Foreign Language Classroom, to be published Aarhus, 1986.

Arndt, H. (forthcoming), 'Speech functions, cooperation and competition in dialogue'.

Austin, J. L. (1962), *How to Do Things with Words*, Oxford, Oxford University Press.

Bazell, G. E., Catford, J. C., Halliday, M. A. K. and Robbins, R. H. (eds) (1966), *In Memory of J. R. Firth*, London, Longman.

Beaugrande, R. de (1980), *Text Discourse and Process*, London, Longman.

Beaugrande, R. de and Dressler, W. (1981), *Introduction to Text Linguistics*, London, Longman; *Einführung in die Textlinguistik*, Tübingen, Niemeyer.

Beekman, J. and Callow, J. (1974), *Translating the Word of God*, Grand Rapids, Michigan, Zondervan Publishing.

Benson, J. D. and Greaves, W. S. (eds) (1985), *Systemic Perspectives on Discourse Vol. 1*, Norwood, N.J., Ablex.

Benveniste, É. (1972), *Problèmes de linguistiques générales*, Paris, Gallimard.

Berry, M. (1981), 'Systematic linguistics and discourse analysis: a multi-layered approach to exchange structure', in Coulthard and Montgomery (eds) (1981: 120–45).

Bloom, L. (1973), *One Word at a Time*, The Hague, Mouton.

Bolinger, D. L. (1972), *Degree Words*, The Hague, Mouton.

Brandt, M. (1975), *The Nature of Causation*, Bloomington, Indiana University Press.

Brook, S. van der, Schlue, K. and Campbell, C. (1980), 'Discourse and second language acquisition of yes/no questions', in Larsen-Freeman (ed.) (1980).

Brown, G. (1977), *Listening to Spoken English*, London, Longman.

Brown, G. and Shadbolt, N. (forthcoming), 'Reference in discourse: the role of indefinite expressions'.

Bruner, J. S. (1975), 'The ontogenesis of speech acts', *Journal of Child Language*, **2**, 1–19.

Bull, W. E. (1971), *Time, Tense and the Verb: A Study in Theoretical and Applied Linguistics, with Particular Attention to Spanish*, Berkeley, University of California Press.

Burt, M. K. and Dulay, H. C. (eds) (1975), *On TESOL '75: New Directions in Second language Learning, Teaching and Bilingual Education*, Washington.

Burton, D. (1981), 'Analysing Spoken Discourse', in Coulthard and Montgomery (eds) (1981).

Catford, J. C. (1968), 'Contrastive analysis and language teaching', in Alatis (ed.) (1968).

Chafe, W. L. (1972), *Meaning and the Structure of Language*, London, University of Chicago Press.

Chafe, W. L. (1982), 'Integration and involvement in speaking, writing and oral literature', in Tannen (ed.) (1982: 20–69).

Chesterman, A. (1977), 'Error analysis and the learner's linguistic repertoire', *Jyväskylä Contrastive Studies*, 4.

Clark, H. H. and Clark, E. V. (1977), *Psychology and Language*, London, Harcourt, Brace, Jovanovich.

Cole, P. (ed.) (1981), *Radical Pragmatics*, London, Academic Press.

Cole, P. and Morgan, J. (eds) (1975), *Syntax and Semantics III: Speech Acts*, New York, Academic Press.

Corder, S. P. (1973), *Introducing Applied Linguistics*, Harmondsworth, Penguin.

—— (1974), 'Error analysis', in Allen and Corder (eds) (1974).

Coulthard, M. (1977), *An Introduction to Discourse Analysis*, London, Longman.

Coulthard, M. and Brazil, D. (1981), 'Exchange structure', in Coulthard and Montgomery (eds) (1981: 83–106).

Coulthard, M and Montgomery, M. (eds) (1981), *Studies in Discourse Analysis*, London, Routledge and Kegan Paul.

Coulthard, M., Montgomery, M. and Brazil, D. (1981), 'Developing a description of spoken discourse', in Coulthard and Montgomery (eds) (1981: 1–50).

Crystal, D. (1966), 'Specification and the English tenses', *Journal of Linguistics*, **2**, 1–34.

Crystal, D. and Davy, D. (1975), *Advanced Conversational English*, London, Longman.

Daneš, F. (ed.) (1974), *Papers on Functional Sentence Perspective*, The Hague, Mouton.

Davidson, D. (1967), 'Causal relations', *Journal of Philosophy*, **64**, 691–73.

Dijk, T. A. van (1977), *Text and Context: Explorations in the Semantics and Pragmatics of Discourse*, London, Longman.

Dijk, T. A. van (1981), *Studies in Pragmatics and Discourse*, The Hague, Mouton.

Dimitrjević, N. R. (1977), 'Problems and implications of contrastive analysis of vocabulary and culture', *Papers and Studies in Contrastive Linguistics*, 4.

Di Pietro, R. (1971), *Language Structures in Contrast*, Rowley, Mass., Newbury House.

Dore, J. (1979), 'Conversational acts and the acquisition of language', in Ochs and Schieffelin (eds) (1979).

Dressler, W. (ed.) (1977), *Current Trends in Textlinguistics*, Berlin, Walter de Gruyter.

Drew, P. (1981), 'Adults' corrections of childrens' Mistakes', in French and Maclure (eds) (1981).

Dubois-Charlier, F. (1975), *Comment s'initier à la linguistique*, Paris, Larousse.

Dulay, H. C. and Burt, M. K. (1972), 'Goofing: an indicator of childrens' second language learning strategies', *Language Learning*, **22**, 2.

Edmondson, W. (1977), *Spoken Discourse: A Model for Analysis*, London, Longman.

Edmondson, W and House, J. (1981), *Let's Talk and Talk about it: A Pedagogic Interactional Grammar of English*, Munich, Urban and Schwarzenberg.

Edwards, D. (1978), 'Social relations and early language', in Lock (ed.) (1978).

Ellis, J. O. (1966), 'On contextual meaning', in Bazell, Catford, Halliday and Robins (eds) (1966).

—— (1966), *Towards a General Comparative Linguistics*, The Hague, Mouton.

—— (1976), 'The role of the concept of text in the elaboration of linguistic data', *York Papers in Linguistics*, 6.

Enkvist, N. E. (1977), 'Stylistics and text linguistics', in Dressler (ed.) (1977).

Enkvist, N. E. (ed.) (1982), *Impromptu Speech: A Symposium*, Abo, Abo Akademi.

Ervin-Tripp, S. (1972), 'On sociolinguistic rules: alteration and co-occurrence', in Gumperz and Hymes (eds) (1972).

Ervin-Tripp, S. and Miller, W. (1977), 'Early discourse: some questions about questions', in Lewis and Rosenblum (eds) (1977).

Faber and Maley (eds) (1980), *Leseverständnis in Fremdsprachenunterricht*, Goethe Institute in conjunction with the British Council.

Faerch, C. and Kasper, G. (1982), 'Phatic, metalingual and metacommunicative functions in discourse: gambits and repairs', in Enkvist (ed.) (1982: 71–103).

Fillmore, C. J. (1971) *Santa Cruz Lectures on Deixis*, Indiana University Linguistics Club.

Fisiak, J. (ed.) (1981), *Contrastive Linguistics and the Language Teacher*, Oxford, Pergammon.

Foss, B. M. (ed.) (1968), *Determinants of Infant Behaviour*, London, Metheun.

French, P. and MacLure, M. (1979), 'Getting the Right Answer and Getting the Answer Right' *Research in Education*, 22, 1–23.

French, P. and MacLure, M. (eds) (1981), *Adult–Child Conversation*, London, Croom Helm.

Garvey, C. (1975), 'Requests and Responses in childrens' speech', *Journal of Child Language*, 2, 41–63.

Givón, T. (ed.) (1979), *Syntax and Semantics 12: Discourse and Syntax*, New York, Academic Press.

Gleason, H. (1968), 'Contrastive analysis in discourse structure', in Alatis (ed.) (1968).

Greenbaum, S. (1969), *Studies in English Adverbial Usage*, London, Longman.

Grice, H. P. (1975), 'Logic and conversation', in Cole and Morgan (eds) (1975).

Grimes, J. (1975), *The Thread of Discourse*, The Hague, Mouton.

Gumperz, J. and Hymes, D. (eds) (1972), *Directions in Sociolinguistics*, London, Holt, Rinehart and Winston.

Halliday, M. A. K. and Hasan, R. (1976), *Cohesion in English*, London, Longman.

Hartmann, R. R. K. (1976), 'Über die Grenzen der kontrastiven lexikologie', in Moser (ed.) (1976: 181–99).

—— (1980), *Contrastive Textology: Comparative Discourse Analysis in Applied Linguistics*, Heidelberg, Groos.

Hasan, R. (1977), 'Text in the systemic-functional model', in Dressler (ed.) (1977).

Hatim, B. (1984), 'A text-typological approach to syllabus design in advanced language teaching', *The Incorporated Linguist*, 23, 3.

—— (forthcoming), 'Discourse analysis in applied linguistics: towards a definition of text variation'.

Hausmann, F. J. (1977), *Einführung in die Benutzung der neufranzösischen Wörterbücher*, Tübingen, Niemeyer.

Hawkins, J. A. (1978), *Definiteness and Indefiniteness*, London, Croom Helm.

Hinds, J. (1982), 'Japanese conversational structures', *Lingua 57*, 301–26.

Hobar, D. (ed.) (1977), *Papers of the Dictionary Society of North America*, Terre Haute, Indiana, DSNA.

Hockett, C. F. (1958), *A Course in Modern Linguistics*, New York, Macmillan.

Hoey, M. (1983), *On the Surface of Discourse*, London, George Allen and Unwin.

Hofland, K. and Johansson, S. (1982) *Word Frequencies in British and American English*, Bergen, Norwegian Computing Centre for the Humanities.

Jacobson, S. (1978), *On the Use, Meaning and Syntax of English Preverbal Adverbials*, Stockholm, Almqvist and Wiksell.

James, C. (1981), 'The transfer of communicative competence', in Fisiak (ed.) (1981).

—— (1983), *Contrastive Analysis*, London, Longman.

Janicki, K. (1977), 'On the feasibility of pedagogical contrastive sociolinguistics' *Papers and Studies in Contrastive Linguistics*, 6, Poznan.

Jensen, K. B. (1980), *A Comparison of Newspaper Reports and Editorials: Towards an Analysis of Coherence Structures*, unpublished M.A. thesis, Aarhus.

Johansson, S. (1978), 'Studies of error gravity', *Acta Universitatis Gothoburgensis*, Gothenburg.

Johansson, S., Leech, G. N. and Goodluck, H. (1978), *Manual of Information to Accompany the Lancaster–Oslo/Bergen Corpus of British English*, Oslo, Department of English, Oslo University.

Johns, T. (1980), 'The text and its messages: approach to the teaching of reading strategies for students of development administration', in Faber and Maley (eds) (1980).

Jordan, M. P. (1978), *The Principal Semantics of the Nominals 'This' and 'That' in Contemporary English Writing*, Ph.D. thesis, Hatfield Polytechnic.

—— (1984), *Rhetoric of Everyday English Texts*, London, George Allen and Unwin.

Kaye, K. and Charney, R. (1981), 'Conversational asymmetry between mothers and children', *Journal of Child Language*, 8, 35–49.

Keenan, E. O. and Schieffelin, B. B. (1976), 'Topic as a discourse notion: a study of topic in the conversations of children and adults', in Li (ed.) (1976).

Kintsch, W., Kosminsky, E., Streby, W. H., McKoon, G. and Keenan, J. R. (1975), 'Comprehension and recall of text as a function of context variables', *Journal of Verbal Learning and Verbal Behaviour*, 14, 196–214.

Kintsch, W. and van Dijk, T. A. (1978), 'Towards a model of text comprehension and production', *Psychological Review*, 85, No. 5, 363–94.

Kintsch, W. and Vipond (1979), 'Reading comprehension and readability in educational practice and psychological theory', in Nilsson (ed.) (1979: 329–65).

Kroch, A and Hindle, D. (1982), 'A quantitative study of the syntax of speech and writing', *Final Report to the National institute of Education*, Grant No. G78–0169.

Lado, R. (1957), *Linguistics across Cultures*, Ann Arbor, Michigan.

Lakoff, R. (1974), 'Remarks on *This* and *That*', *CLS Papers*, 10, 345–56.

Larsen-Freeman, D. (ed.) (1980), *Discourse Analysis in Second Language Research*, Rowley, Mass., Newbury House.

Laver, J. and Hutcheson, S. (eds) (1972), *Communication in Face-to-Face Interaction*, Harmondsworth, Penguin.

Leech, G. and Svartvik, J. (1975), *A Communicative Grammar of English*, London, Longman.

Lee, W. R. (1968), 'Thoughts on contrastive linguistics in the context of language teaching', in Alatis (ed.) (1968).

Leisi, E. (1953), *Der Wortinhalt: Seine Struktur im Deutschen und Englischen*, Heidelberg, Quelle and Meyer.

Levenston, E. A. (1971), 'Over-indulgence and under-representation: aspects of mother-tongue interference', in Nickel (ed.) (1971).

Levinson, S. C. (1980), 'Speech act theory: the state of the art', *Language Teaching and Linguistics: Abstracts*, 13, 5–24.

Lewes, M. and Rosenblum, L. (eds) (1977), *The Origins of Behaviour: Interaction, Conversation, and the Development of Languages*, New York, Wiley.

Li, C. (ed.) (1976), *Subject and Topic*, New York, Academic Press.

Li, C. and Thompson, S. A. (1976), 'Subject and topic: a new typology of language', in Li (ed.) (1976: 457–89).

Lock, A. (ed.) (1978), *Action, Gesture and Symbol*, London, Academic Press.

Lyons, J. (1977), *Semantics* London, Cambridge University Press.

Lyons, J. (1979), 'Deixis and anaphora', in Myers (ed.) (1979: 88–103).

MacLure, M. (1981), *Making Sense of Children's Talk: Structure and Strategy in Adult–Child Conversation*, PH.D. thesis, University of York.

McTear, M. (1981), 'The development of conversation in pre-school children', unpublished dissertation, Ulster Polytechnic.

Marton, W. (1968). 'Equivalence and congruence in transformational contrastive studies', *Studia Anglica Poznaniensia*, 1.

Mehan, H. (1978), 'Structuring school structure', *Harvard Educational Review*, 48, No. 1, 32–64.

Monaghan, J. (1985), 'On the signalling of complete thoughts', in Benson and Greaves (eds) (1985: 373–82).

Meser, H. (ed.) (1976), *Probleme der Lexikologie und der Lexikographie*, Düsseldorf, Schwann.

Myers, T. (ed.) (1979), *The Development of Conversation and Discourse*, Edinburgh.

Newson, J and Newson, E. (1975), 'Intersubjectivity and the transmission of culture: on the social origins of symbolic functioning', *Bulletin of the British Psychological Society*, 25, 437–46.

Nickel, G. (ed.) (1971), *Papers in Contrastive Linguistics*, London, Cambridge University Press.

Nilsson, L. G. (ed.) (1979), *Memory Processes and Problems*, Hillsdale, N.J., Erlbaum.

Nöth, W. (1977), 'The semiotic framework of textlinguistics', in Dressler (ed.) (1977).

Ochs, E. (1979), 'Planned and unplanned discourse', in Givón (ed.) (1979: 51–80).

Ochs, E., Schieffelin, B. B. and Platt, M. (1979), 'Propositions across utterances and speakers', in Ochs and Schieffelin (eds) (1979).

Ochs, E. and Schieffelin, B. B. (eds) (1979), *Developmental Pragmatics*, New York, Academic Press.

Oh, C.-K. and Dineen, D. (eds) (1979), *Syntax and Semantics II: Presuppositions*, New York, Academic Press.

Petterson, T. (ed.) (1979), *Papers from the Fifth Scandinavian Conference of Linguistics*, Stockholm.

Politzer, R. L. (1972), *Linguistics and Applied Linguistics: Aims and Methods*, Center for Curriculum Development, Philadelphia.

Pomerantz, A. (1978), 'Compliment responses: notes on the cooperation of multiple constraints', in Schenkein (ed.) (1978).

Prince, E. F. (1981), 'Toward a taxonomy of given–new information', in Cole (ed.) (1981).

Quirk, R. (1954), *The Concessive Relation in Old English Poetry*, New Haven, Yale University Press.

Quirk, R., Greenbaum, S., Leech, G. N. and Svartvik, J. (1972), *A Grammar of Contemporary English*, London, Longman.

Richards, M. P. M. (ed.) (1974), *The Integration of a Child into a Social World*, Cambridge, Cambridge University Press.

Richards, J. C. (1975), 'The context for error analysis', in Burt and Dulay (eds) (1975).

Richards, J. C. and Sukwiwat, M. (1983), 'Language transfer and conversational competence', *Applied Linguistics*, 4, No. 2.

Riley, P. (1981), 'Towards a contrastive pragmalinguistics', in Fisiak (ed.) (1981).

Ryan, J. (1974), 'Early language development: towards a communicative analysis', in Richards (ed.) (1974).

Sacks, H., Schegloff, E. A. and Jefferson, G. (1974), 'A simplest systematics for the organization of turn-taking in conversation', *Language*, 50, 696–735.

Sajavaara, K. (1977), 'Contrastive linguistics past and present and a communicative approach, *Jyväskylä Contrastive Studies*, 4.

Sawyers, R. *et al.* (1982), *Harrap's Concise German and English Dictionary*, London, Harrap.

Schachter, J. (1974), 'An error in error analysis', *Language Learning'*, 24, No. 2.

Schegloff, E. (1968), 'Sequencing in conversational openings', *American Anthropologist*, 70, No. 4, 1075–95, and in Laver and Hutcheson (eds) (1972).

—— (1982), 'Discourse as an interactional achievement: some uses of 'uh huh' and other things that come between sentences', in Tannen (ed.) (1982: 71–93).

Schegloff, E. and Sachs, H. (1974), 'Opening up closings', in Turner (ed.) (1974).

Schegloff, E. A., Jefferson, G. and Sacks, H. (1977), 'The preference for self-correction in the organization of repair in conversation', *Language*, 53, 361–82.

Schenkein, J. (ed.) (1978), *Studies in the Organization of Conversational Interaction*, New York, Academic Press.

Searle, J. R. (1975), 'Indirect Speech Acts' in Cole and Morgan (eds) (1975).

—— (1976), 'A classification of illocutionary Acts', *Language and Society*, 5.

Shotter, J. (1978), 'The cultural context of communication studies: theoretical and methodological issues', in Lock (ed.) (1978).

Sinclair, J and Coulthard, R. M. (1975), *Towards an Analysis of Discourse: The English Used by Teachers and Pupils*, London, Oxford University Press.

Smith, N. and Wilson, D. (1979), *Modern Linguistics: The Results of Chomsky's Revolution*, Harmondsworth, Penguin.

Snow, C. E. (1977), 'The development of conversation between mothers and babies' *Journal of Child Language*, 4, 1–22.

Steiner, R. J. (1977), 'How a bilingual dictionary best serves the writer', in Hobar (ed.) (1977: 24–31).

Stemmer, B. (1981), *Kohäsion im gesprochenen Diskurs deutscher Lerner des Englishchen*, Bochum.

Stenström A.-B. (1982), 'Feedback', in Enkvist (ed.) (1982: 319–40).

Strang, B. M.H. (1962), *Modern English Structure*, London, Edward Arnold.

Stubbs, M. (1981), 'Motivating analyses of exchange structure' in Coulthard and Montgomery (eds) (1981: 107–19).

Svartvik, J. and Quirk, R. (1976), *A Corpus of Spoken English*, Lund, CWK Gleerup.

—— (1980), *A Corpus of English Conversation*, Lund, CWK Gleerup.

Svartvik, J., Eeg-Olofsson, M. Forsheden, O., Oreström B. and Thavenius, C. (1982), *Survey of Spoken English: Report on Research 1975–81*, Lund, Gleerup.

Tannen, D. (ed.) (1982), *Analyzing Discourse: Text and Talk*, Washington, D.C. Georgetown University Press.

Tannen, D. (ed.) (1982), *Exploring Orality and Literacy*, Norwood, N.J., Ablex.

Terrell, P. *et al.* (1980), *Collins German–English, English–German Dictionary*, London and Glasgow, Collins.

Thomas, J. (1983), 'Cross-cultural pragmatic failure', *Applied Linguistics*, 4 No. 2.

Tottie, G. and Paradis, C. (1982), 'From function to structure: some pragmatic determinants of syntactic frequencies in impromptu speech', in Enkvist (ed.) (1982: 307–17).

Tottie, G., Altenberg, B. and Hermeren, L. (1983), *English in Speech and Writing: A Manual for Students*, ETOS Report 1, Lund, Department of English, Lund University.

Trevarthen, C., Hubley, P. and Sheeran, L. (1975), 'Psychological Actions in Early Infancy', *La Recherche*, 6, 447–58.

Turner, R. (ed.) (1974), *Ethnomethodology*, Harmondsworth, Penguin.

Weinreich, U. (1953), *Languages in Contact*, New York.

Weinrich, H. (1964), *Tempus: Besprochene und erzählte Welt*, Stuttgart, Kohlhammer.

Wells, C. G. (ed.) (1981), *Learning through Interaction*, Cambridge, Cambridge University Press.

Werlich, E. (1976), *A Text Grammar of English*, Heidelberg, Quelle and Meyer.

Werner, R. (1982), 'Zur Reihenfolge der Definitionen bzw: Übersetzungsäquivalente im Wörterbuchartikel', *Lebende Sprachen*, 27, 150–6.

Wiegand, H. E. (forthcoming), Überlegungen zu einer Theorie der lexikographischen Sprachbeschreibung', Copenhagen Colloquium.

Wilson, D. and Sperber, D. (1979), 'Ordered entailments: an alternative to presuppositional theory', in Oh and Dinneen (eds) (1979).

Winter, E. O. (1971), 'Connection in science material: a proposition about the semantics of clause relations', in *C.I.L.T. Reports and Papers, No. 7: Science and Technology in a Second Language*, London, Centre for Information on Language Teaching and Research, 41–52.

—— (1974), *Replacement as a function: a study of some of its principal features in the clause relations of contemporary English*, Ph.D. thesis, University of London.

—— (1976), *Fundamentals of information structure: a pilot manual for further development according to student need*, mimeo, Hatfield Polytechnic.

—— (1977), 'A clause-relational approach to English texts: a study of some predictive lexical in written discourse'. Special Issue, *Instructional Science*, 6, No. 1, 1–92.

—— (1979), 'Replacement as a fundamental function of the sentence in context', *Forum Linguisticum*, 4, No. 2, 95–133.

—— (1982), *Towards a Contextual Grammar Of English*, London, George Allen and Unwin.

Wolff, P. H. (1968), 'The natural history of crying and other vocalization in early infancy', in Foss (ed.) (1968).

Wootton, A. (forthcoming), 'The managing of grantings and rejections by parents in request sequences', *Semiotica*.

Wright, W. (1955), *A Grammar of the Arabic Language*, Cambridge, Cambridge University Press.

Zgusta, L. (1971), *Manual of Lexicography*, The Hague, Mouton.

Index